TAXING AND SPENDING

For Ranse –

Joe Pileggi

TAXING AND

SPENDING

ALABAMA'S BUDGET IN TRANSITION

Joseph C. Pilegge, Jr.

Published for the Bureau of Public Administration,
The University of Alabama, by
THE UNIVERSITY OF ALABAMA PRESS
university, alabama

Library of Congress Cataloging in Publication Data

Pilegge, Joseph
  Taxing and spending, Alabama's budget in transition.

  Bibliography: p.
  Includes index.
  1. Budget—Alabama. 2. Revenue—Alabama.
  3. Alabama—Appropriations and expenditures.
  4. Program budgeting—Alabama. I. Title.
  HJ2053.A2P54   353.9′761′00722   78-17155
  ISBN 0-8173-4839-5

Contents

Tables

Figures

Preface

The past decade has witnessed an unprecedented expansion in the role of governments at all levels in the United States. Nowhere has this expansion, with its attendant increases in public expenditures, been more evident than among our fifty state governments. Alabama has not been exempt. In the years between 1960 and 1975, while the state's population increased a mere 11 percent, the costs of providing governmental services rose by more than 360 percent. Even allowing for the inroads of inflation, the increase in the cost of state government was more than ten times that in the population.

Alabama's policy makers, like their counterparts throughout the nation, found themselves locked into an escalating pattern of public expenditures for old programs oriented toward problems of the past. Commitments to ongoing programs, the statutory earmarking of a high percentage of existing revenues, constitutional restrictions on borrowing, and public opposition to new or increased taxes, all combined to restrain the state's ability to respond to new priorities and created a crisis in public financial management.

Faced with a choice between two unattractive alternatives—raising taxes or reducing state services—officials in the executive and legislative branches of government sought a third option: utilizing existing fiscal resources more effectively. This book is concerned with a major part of that effort.

Traditionally, Alabama employed a classic object-of-expenditure budget, a form of presentation that depicted in great detail those things that government bought. It provided little information about what was done by the agencies being funded. Standing alone, an itemization of the amounts to be spent for salaries, travel, telephones, supplies, and equipment does little to aid understanding of what government is trying to accomplish. The conversion to a program-type budget in the mid-1970s has required that proposed outlays of state funds be linked to governmental goals and to specific services provided by the agencies seeking the money. Eventually, performance data will be developed to measure the success or failure of programs designed to serve the state's citizens.

While this book focuses on the budgetary process, or the expenditure side of public finance, it also devotes some attention to the state's revenue system. The kinds of taxes and other income sources utilized by the state government are examined and comparisons are made with revenue structures found elsewhere in the nation, particularly in other southeastern states. Problems associated with both the taxing and spending sides of state finance are discussed along with an assessment of prospects for change.

Budgeting can be an enlightening process. It can reveal situations and conditions within government that might otherwise go unnoticed. Thus, budgetary reform has focused attention on programs that duplicate each other and agencies whose original purposes have long been forgotten but whose legislative mandates remain in effect. The demand for more effective management of fiscal resources has had a rippling effect throughout state government. "Sunset" legislation and proposals for wide-ranging reorganization of state administration are two by-products of budgetary reform dealt with in this study.

It is too early to assess accurately or fairly the effect of budgetary reform on Alabama's fiscal policy or to appraise its impact on state government generally. An evaluation of the first year's experience, however, suggests that the changes instituted in 1976 were more than cosmetic. Whether changes in budgetary forms and processes produce real changes in outcomes is a much-debated point. While it is not yet possible to arrive at any firm conclusions about the Alabama experience, it would be surprising indeed if such far-reaching alterations failed to have a significant impact on how the state's financial resources are used.

Budgeting is not often the subject of drawing room conversation. Nor do books on the subject usually qualify as recreational reading. This brief volume, while maintaining the expected level of sobriety, seeks to deal with a highly complex and technical topic in a manner that will not discourage the general reader. Formal training in accounting, law, or public administration is not a prerequisite for understanding the material in this book.

Authorship is seldom a solitary affair. Too many persons contributed to the development of this work to list them all. But I especially want to note the assistance of two colleagues, Professors L. Franklin Blitz and James D. Thomas of the political science department of The University of Alabama. They read early versions of the study and offered useful suggestions along the way. Donald S. Vaughan of the University of Mississippi also contributed helpful criticisms at a crucial stage of the writing. And Paula Franks cheerfully tolerated my numerous revisions while providing the typing assistance without which the manuscript could not have come into being.

Finally, I want to acknowledge the financial support provided by the Bureau of Public Administration. The University of Alabama maintains the bureau for the study of public problems, but no conclusions regarding the university's policies should be drawn from this study. The author, of course, accepts sole responsibility for the accuracy of the material presented and the soundness of his interpretations and analysis.

Tuscaloosa, Alabama   JOSEPH C. PILEGGE, JR.
September, 1977

1

The Budget: An Introduction

Budgeting—the formal presentation and adoption of a financial plan of action—is a relatively recent development in the United States. For all practical purposes, it is a creature of the twentieth century, having emerged from the municipal-reform movement of seventy-five years ago.

The modern system of budgeting owes its existence to two major changes in American political and economic life. First, the growth of institutions of representative government was accompanied by citizen demands for accountability on the part of those holding public office. Second, the rapid expansion of governmental activity led to the realization that this activity had an important impact on the economy.

Americans, long blessed with material abundance and revenues that consistently outran expenditures, came to the use of budgets in government later than most nations. Both Great Britain and France, for example, had adopted fairly sophisticated budget systems prior to the American Civil War.[1]

Budgeting by governments in the United States appeared first at the local level. It was at this level, beginning around the turn of the century, that the costs of government first began to outrun available revenues. And it was also at this level that the attacks of reform groups against "invisible," unaccountable, and sometimes corrupt governments had their initial impact.

Following the lead of some of the nation's larger cities, state governments between 1910 and 1920 moved rapidly to adopt budget systems. By 1921, when Congress enacted the nation's first budget law, more than forty states were using such a system.

The states had not adopted budgeting earlier primarily because they had not faced serious financial trouble before the turn of the century. In the years preceding 1900, the total expenditures of all state governments combined amounted to less than $200 million a year—that is, an amount about one-tenth the present annual outlays for the state of Alabama alone.

Budgeting is an instrument for coping with scarcity. It becomes necessary to adopt a financial plan only when available funds fall short of meeting the demands made upon them. As the costs of government began to increase, tax-payer groups called for "economy and efficiency" in the public sector. A formal budget, prepared by the chief executive and submitted to the legislature for approval, was seen as a means of reaching that goal.

There are many types of budgets, and the process by which they are developed varies greatly from one place to another. Basically, however, a budget is a formal plan, expressed in financial terms, constituting an estimate of how an organization intends to spend money in accomplishing its purposes over a stated period of time.

While budgets can take many different forms, all make an effort to present a more or less comprehensive picture of the organization's financial planning. Both income (revenues) and outgo (expenditures) are usually presented.

It should be kept in mind that budget figures relating to revenues and expenditures are only estimates and, as such, rarely match precisely the amounts that are actually taken in and paid out. In Alabama, where the state budget formerly covered a two-year period, estimates of income and outgo had to be made some thirty months prior to the end of the fiscal period that they covered.

Changes in economic conditions, unforeseen new demands on government, and an almost infinite number of unanticipated developments can intervene to alter revenues, expenditures, or both. The impact of inflation in recent years, for example, has greatly increased state-government costs. On the other hand, a sagging economy that increases unemployment and decreases personal and business incomes will result in some decline in state revenues. Income from gasoline taxes, for example, fell sharply during the Arab oil embargo of 1973–1974.

The inability of state governments to control political and economic developments that may adversely affect them places even greater importance upon the ability to estimate accurately future costs and income. Also, unlike the national government, the states do not possess virtually unlimited borrowing powers with which to compensate for an excess of expenditures over revenues. The extended time period involved in state budgeting, the lack of control over national and international events, and restrictions on indebtedness are just a few of the problems that make state budgeting difficult.

At all levels of government, budgeting is a part of the broader political decision-making process. Although there is a tendency to view budgeting as a technical matter, it is in fact deeply infused with political considerations. If the central question of politics is, "Who gets what, and how much?", the budget records the policy response to that question. Few programs or policies of government can be carried on without money. Since in modern societies the demands on government for programs benefitting particular segments of the population greatly exceed the resources available, there is constant conflict over whose preferences will prevail. The outcome of this conflict is reflected in the budget allocations for various activities.[2]

It is through the budget process that governments establish their priorities. The rhetoric of politics, the promises made during campaigns, or other public statements, are poor guides to the policy intentions of those in public office. The budget is a more accurate scorecard; it reflects the many compromises among contending interest groups, governmental agencies, and elected officials that are necessary in arriving at public policy in a democracy.

The budget is, then, "political" in that it shows with some precision just who has gained and who has lost (and to what extent) in the competition for scarce resources. An examination of the amounts appropriated for a particular agency or program over a period of years will reveal the relative success it has had in the battle for public and political support.

There is more to budgeting, however, than the mere existence of a document. Indeed, most studies of budgeting tend to focus primarily on the *process* by which the budget comes into being. And that will be our main concern.

In examining the budget process in Alabama state government, it is necessary to look first at the history of its development since the beginning of this century. Budgeting is an evolutionary process and the system being used today bears only a faint resemblance to that of earlier periods. Although our emphasis will be on the budget process, a separate chapter will discuss some characteristics of the budget. Alabama has employed the traditional line-item budget, but recent modification of this form in the direction of program budgeting will be reviewed in detail in the final chapter.

Much of the material will be concerned with identifying and explaining the roles of the many participants in the budget process. The number of persons involved in preparing, authorizing, and executing the budget runs into the hundreds. Our account will concentrate on the key actors, ranging from the individual agency budget officers to the governor and his staff aides. The role of the legislature, with its constitutional "power of the purse," also will be treated. A separate chapter will examine trends in revenues and expenditures, noting in particular the types of taxes utilized and comparing Alabama's revenue effort with that of other states in the region and the nation.

The final phase of any budget process is that of auditing expenditures made during the fiscal year. This is required in order to ensure that state funds have been spent legally— that is, according to the intent of the laws under which money was appropriated—and that such expenditures have been properly documented. Here, too, there have been some recent changes in approach, especially in moving from a strict-accounting basis to an examination of the overall performance of government agencies.

Budgeting is a cyclical activity with some phase of the process going on at all times, resulting in what might be called a "calendar" of budgetary activity. In tracing the events on this calendar, it is obvious that budgeting is a function that involves extensive participation by members of the executive and legislative branches of government.

Basically, the steps are as follows: budget preparation by the executive; budget authorization—the approval of appropriations—by the legislature; budget execution or implementation, an executive branch responsibility; and, finally, the postaudit, primarily a function of the legislature or an agency designated by it. All these steps, as they apply to the Alabama state budget, will be reviewed in the pages that follow.

During the mid-1970s, Alabama's budget procedures, essentially unchanged for more than a quarter of a century, came under intensive examination by those within and outside of state government. Several study commissions and legislative committees found the financial management system wanting and recommended a variety of measures to improve its performance.[3] The product of this activity was the enactment in 1976 of a comprehensive budget-reform bill that, along with other related actions such as the adoption of annual legislative sessions, passage of a "Sunset" law, and reorganization of the legislature's fiscal staff structure, promised to alter drastically the state's traditional approach to budgeting public funds. All these developments will be treated in the following chapters. First, however, a look backward, beginning with the Constitutional Convention of 1901, where concern about the state's smoldering fiscal problems first received official attention.

2

Historical Development

In May, 1901, as delegates to the Alabama Constitutional Convention met in Montgomery, the state's indebtedness had swollen to $9.3 million. This debt, a sizeable sum for those times, was largely the result of the inability of the legislature to match the amount of its appropriations with available state revenues.

There was no central budgeting authority in state government. The legislature met infrequently and the estimates of anticipated revenues it received from executive officials were not much more than guesses. Expenditures were authorized that, in the aggregate, usually exceeded the state's income for the year.

It was not surprising, therefore, that the principal concern of many delegates was to provide a constitutional mechanism for balancing the budget. More accurate estimates of income were to be coupled with strict limitations on the legislature's appropriating authority.

In essence, the constitution of 1901 attacked the problem in two ways. First, it virtually prohibited creation of new debt and restricted the short-term bank debt of the state to $300,000. Second, it prescribed that the legislature could not appropriate an amount in excess of the estimated revenues for any fiscal year. Further, the legislature was no longer to make its own revenue estimates, but was to be guided by estimates prepared by a board consisting of the state auditor, the treasurer, and the governor.

The new constitution required that the governor present to the legislature a general revenue bill based upon these estimates of income. This feature provoked some of the most heated debate of the convention. It was criticized on the ground that it violated the separation of powers principle by injecting the governor and other executive-branch officials into the legislative process. Others saw more sinister intent in the governor's power to recommend the details of a general-revenue bill. Delegate John W. A. Sanford of Montgomery argued that the provision was "monarchical" and represented a return to "the very principles from which our forefathers revolted." Delegate Thomas L. Long of Walker County went even further: "We are giving the Governor and Auditor of Alabama more power than the Czar of Russia," he declared.[1]

Defenders of the proposal, led by former Governor William C. Oates, prevailed. It was their contention that only the auditor and governor possessed sufficient information on which to project the state's revenues. The legislature, Oates argued, had consistently failed in this task, and its failure had led to the accumulation of the large state debt.

Unfortunately, the convention gave less attention to the problem of managing the state's expenditures than it did to trying to deal with the revenue problem. It should be kept in mind, however, that at this time no state had as yet adopted a budget system. Indeed, it was to be another fifteen years before Maryland put into effect what is generally regarded as the first executive budget.

The Early Failures

In spite of, or perhaps because of, the language of the constitution, Alabama's fiscal affairs were to remain in disarray. The prohibition against new debt was circumvented through the issuance of interest-bearing certificates of indebtedness. These warrants were presented to banks by the state treasurer, who prepaid the interest from a special contingency fund of $100,000. The legislature continued to disregard the requirement for a balanced budget, making little effort to correlate its revenues and expenditures. Revenue estimates presented by the auditor and governor were generally ignored. As a result, the budget was not balanced for any fiscal year between 1907 and 1932, by which time the state's deficit had climbed to nearly $20 million.[2]

Few efforts were made during this long period to improve the budget system. In 1919 the legislature created an *ex officio* budget commission consisting of the governor, the attorney general, and the auditor. Later, the chief examiner of accounts, the state treasurer, the commissioner of agriculture and industries, and the chairman of the state Tax Commission were added. This law was defective in that it only authorized the submission of a budget proposal to the legislature. It gave the governor no authority to implement the budget once appropriation bills had been passed. The Budget Commission became inactive after 1927. Its staff having been disbanded, it made no attempt to submit revenue and expenditure estimates for the four-year budget period beginning in 1931.

The Reforms of 1932

In 1932, following an examination of Alabama's state government, the prestigious Brookings Institution explained the failure of the Budget Commission:

> Its failure to function is apparently due to the attitude of past legislatures toward its recommendations, to the fact that over 80% of all departmental and institutional appropriations are permanent recurring appropriations, and because it is an *ex-officio* body without permanent personnel.[3]

In addition, the state's accounting and reporting system

failed to produce adequate information on which to base revenue and expenditure estimates. "It is common knowledge," the Brookings report concluded, "that the state's financial records and reports for a number of years have not developed complete information regarding the financial condition and operation of the government."[4]

In the wake of such findings, Governor B.M. Miller called the legislature into special session in August, 1932. The purpose of the session was to deal with the problem of continuing deficits and inadequate budget authority. The result was enactment of the Budget and Financial Control Act of 1932, popularly known as the "Fletcher Act."[5] This act abolished the *ex-officio* Budget Commission and placed responsibility for submitting the budget in the governor. In addition, it created the office of state comptroller and vested in that office a wide variety of financial duties, including that of preparing the budget document for the governor.

The new law, which is still the basic legal foundation for state budgeting, provided Alabama with an executive budget system similar to those that had developed in other states. It required the governor to submit a balanced budget to the legislature, along with his budget message setting forth his program for meeting the state's expenditure needs for the ensuing four years. (Prior to 1943, the legislature met in regular session only once every four years.) In addition to proposing appropriations for each organizational unit of state government, the governor was required to submit drafts of appropriations bills to be acted upon by the legislature.

The act prescribed six basic steps in formulating and presenting the budget:

1. All organization units were required to submit to the state comptroller estimates of their spending needs for each of the four fiscal years.

2. The comptroller was required to submit, not later than

October 1, an estimate of the total income of the government for the quadrennium.

3. By November 1 the comptroller was to have prepared a tentative budget for submission to the governor.

4. The governor, after receiving the tentative budget, was to arrange for public hearings. These hearings, to be held not later than December, were to be attended by departmental officers, the governor-elect, the comptroller, and the chairmen of the appropriations committees of the two houses of the legislature.

5. Following his inauguration in January, the new governor was to formulate the final version of the budget. In this, he was not bound by the decisions taken by the outgoing governor or comptroller, but could make whatever alterations he deemed advisable.

6. The final step was submission of the budget to the legislature not later than February 15 of each quadrennial session.

In setting forth this schedule, it should be kept in mind that, until changed by constitutional amendment in 1939, the legislature convened in regular session on the second Tuesday in January. Between 1943 and 1976, the regular working sessions began on the first Tuesday in May. Beginning in 1977, under legislation enacted in 1976, the legislature was to convene on the first Tuesday in February during the first three years of the legislative term, and in the fourth (election) year, the regular session was to open on the second Tuesday in January.[6]

While the Budget and Financial Control Act of 1932 provided a fairly comprehensive budget system, it had at least two basic weaknesses. First, because of the need to budget for four-year periods, the comptroller was faced with making revenue and expenditure estimates based on information gathered five years prior to the end of the fiscal period. Second, the legislative sessions were held concurrently with the taking of office by a newly elected governor. Therefore, the incoming governor had only about one month after inauguration to study the tentative budget and put the document into final form.

Amendments of 1939

This procedure remained in effect until 1939, when two events occurred to alter the arrangement. First, the voters approved the 39th Amendment to the state constitution providing for biennial sessions of the legislature and shifting the convening dates from January to May. Second, the legislature approved certain amendments to the Fletcher Act that changed the timetable for budget preparation and submission. With the legislature not scheduled to meet until early May, the deadlines noted above were moved ahead approximately four months. Income and expenditure estimates, previously required by October 1, were now due by February 1. The tentative budget was to be presented by March 1 rather than by November 1. And, more importantly, the governor was given until mid-April to call public hearings on the budget. This allowed an incoming governor, taking office in January, ample time to put his personal stamp upon the budget document. Of course, the entire budget process was now placed on a biennial basis—that is, budgeting was for a two-year period rather than for four years as in the past.

Of equal importance, the legislature abolished the independent office of state comptroller and replaced it with a new Department of Finance.[7] Within the new department, a Division of the Budget was created to be headed by the state budget officer. Most of the functions of the comptroller were transferred to the Budget Division along with the granting of additional powers for budget preparation and execution. What remained of the comptroller's duties, largely in the areas of accounting, auditing and statistical reporting, was placed in the Control and Accounts Division within the

Finance Department. Additional modifications related to the handling of earmarked receipts and the allotment of appropriated funds.

The Question of Control

As a result of the 1939 amendments to the budget act, the incoming administration became responsible for preparation of the budget. Originally, most of the work in formulating the budget had been done by the outgoing governor and his comptroller. The incoming administration was prevented by the short time available from making substantial alterations. Since 1939, a new governor has had nearly five months to prepare the budget that he submits to the legislature in May. (One consequence of moving the convening date of regular sessions to February, beginning in 1977, was to negate this advantage). Finally, the 1939 action provided for budgeting for a two-year time period, a more manageable span for making income and expenditure estimates than the four-year period previously used.

These amendments, along with the law creating the new Department of Finance headed by a director appointed by the governor, were designed to give the state's chief executive greater control over fiscal affairs. There is, of course, frequently a gap between legislative intent and subsequent implementation of policy. This was true in the case of the budget. Although the provisions of the Budget and Financial Control Act could be applied to all state agencies except the Department of Agriculture, the legislature did not insist upon it. As a result, many agencies continued to operate outside the provisions of the act until 1949. In that year, the legislature, led by a so-called "economy bloc," acted to restrict agency independence by imposing legislative ceilings on the expenditures of nearly all state agencies.[8]

It should not be construed from this, however, that effective budgetary control is exercised by either the governor or the legislature over all the expenditures of state government. Such is far from the case. Although all state agencies are subject to the "budget process," control by the governor and the legislature is essentially limited to appropriations from the General Fund and, to a more limited extent, those contained in the Special Educational Trust Fund. During the mid-1970s expenditures from the General Fund accounted for less than 10 percent of total state spending. Adding expenditures from the education fund increased the proportion to 45 to 50 percent of state expenditures. Thus, approximately 50 percent of state spending escapes close scrutiny or substantial modification as a result of decisions made by the governor or legislature.

Two factors are chiefly responsible for this situation. First, the practice of "earmarking" revenues—setting aside by law the receipts from particular taxes or fees for specific use—is widespread. One study published in 1969 estimated that more than 80 percent of Alabama's revenues were earmarked.[9] The second factor minimizing budgetary control is the relatively heavy dependence upon federal grants-in-aid. Most federal-grant money is also designated for specific uses and can not be utilized for any other purposes. According to census figures, federal aid accounts for more than 25 percent of total state revenues in Alabama. It should be kept in mind that tax receipts paid into the Special Educational Trust Fund are earmarked in the sense that the money may not be used for purposes unrelated to education. However, allocation among the various educational institutions and activities is subject to decisions made by the governor and legislature.

Recent Changes

In an effort to improve its ability to cope with an expanding state budget, the legislature in 1975 created the Legislative Fiscal Office.[10] This new office, modeled after the Congressional Office of the Budget, is responsible for gathering information, compiling statistical data, and submitting estimates and appraisals regarding revenue and expenditure matters. Headed by a director who serves at the pleasure of the legislature, the fiscal office staff is directly responsible to a newly created Joint Fiscal Committee. Members of the joint committee include the chairmen and three additional members from both the House Ways and Means Committee and the Senate Finance and Taxation Committee. The lieutenant governor and the Speaker of the House also serve as members of the committee during their terms.

This action, about which more will be said later, represents one of several changes in the budget process during the 1975/76 biennium. Certain procedures have been clarified and an effort has been made to bring the proposed budgets of all state agencies into the review process. Additional controls have been instituted in the budget execution phase, particularly by subjecting all agencies to the allotment process. This means that the agencies, rather than receiving the full amount of their annual appropriations in a single lump sum, receive funds allocated by the Budget Division on a quarterly basis throughout the year.

On June 10, 1975, the voters approved a constitutional amendment authorizing annual sessions of the legislature.[11] In the long run, this action could prove to be more helpful in improving the budget process than anything done in the past quarter of a century.

In the closing days of its 1976 regular session, the legislature enacted a so-called "zero-base" budgeting bill, the implementation of which would require substantial alterations in both budget process and format.[12] The immediate effect, beginning with preparation of the 1977/78 fiscal-year budget, was to move the state in the direction of program budgeting, a marked departure from its traditional approach to allocating public funds.

Budgeting, like other governmental activities, is largely

the product of an evolutionary process. To understand how it works today it is necessary to examine its development over a period of time. That has been the purpose of this chapter. Two principal points may be made in conclusion: First, the type of executive budget now found in almost all the states came to Alabama relatively late, more than a decade after its adoption by some forty other states. Second, it has been traditional in the state to exempt a large portion of total expenditures from budgetary scrutiny by both the governor and the legislature. Thus, although Alabama has, in a technical sense, an ''executive budget,'' the power of the governor actually to control state expenditures has been limited. Similarly, the legislature is restricted in its ability to establish state spending priorities and to shift funds from one program or department to another. In the mid-1970s, this inflexibility was beginning to create serious problems.

3

The Budgetary Process

Governmental budgeting is a cyclical process. It reflects a sequence of decisions taken over a period of time by a rather large number of administrative and political officials. The phases of the budget cycle can be generally identified as: (1) executive preparation and submission, (2) legislative authorization, (3) execution, and (4) audit. As can be seen, budgeting is an activity in which both the executive and legislative branches are deeply involved.

Executive Preparation

In Alabama, as in most states, the preparation of the budget is primarily a duty of the governor and a staff responsible to him. The law is quite specific in setting forth the governor's role. He must submit a budget that is "to make known in all practical detail the financial condition and operation of the government and the effect that the budget as proposed by him will have on such condition and operation."[1] The budget document, setting forth the governor's financial plan for the next fiscal year, must be presented to the legislature within five days after it convenes in regular session.

To assist the governor in preparing the budget, the legislature created in 1939, within the Department of Finance, a Budget Division headed by the state budget officer. The director of finance, an appointee of the governor, names the

FIGURE 1
Alabama Department of Finance

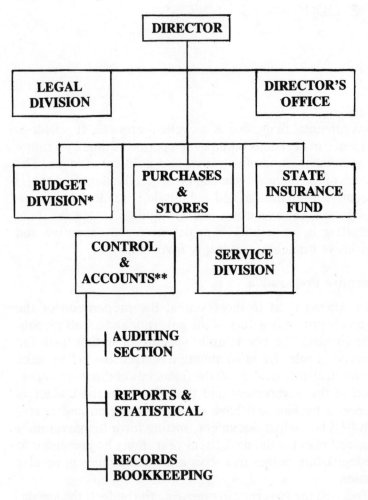

*State Budget Officer heads Division
**State Comptroller Officer heads Division

budget officer subject to the approval of the governor. Thus, there is a direct line of responsibility running from the budget officer, through the director of finance, to the governor.

The Budget Division assembles a tentative budget for the governor, spelling out in considerable detail the proposed expenditures of each department, agency, bureau, board, institution, or other unit of government. In performing this function, the budget officer is authorized to obtain needed information from any agency or office of the government. The Budget Division is also responsible for execution of the budget after its enactment by the legislature. This includes allotment of funds to the various agencies and enforcement of the laws, rules, and regulations relating to the budget.

Through the 1977 fiscal year, Alabama's budget document followed a "line-item" or "object" classification format. This involved the separate listing of expenditures for salaries, equipment purchases, and other expenses, such as supplies, travel, and utilities. Although the terms are used interchangeably in most writing on the subject, there is a fine line of distinction between line-item and object-of-expenditure budgets. The former usually refers to narrowly detailed appropriations, such as individual salaries or specific items of equipment to be purchased. An object classification utilizes more general categories, such as "equipment," "supplies," etc. A second point of distinction rests on the ease or difficulty with which funds can be transferred within the budget. Traditionally, line-items could be altered only with approval of the legislative body, the appropriating authority, while object-type appropriations were subject to modification through executive action. In this sense, Alabama's budget could most accurately be described as an object-classification type. In any event, this format was altered significantly with the adoption of a "zero-base" budget approach in 1976.

Responsibility for initiating the budget process lies with

the governor. However, budgeting is an institutionalized activity in which the first steps are taken by the Budget Division when it issues instructions and forms to the departments some six months prior to the convening of the legislature. Spending estimates prepared by major subdivisions of each agency are filtered upward and aggregated by department. In the past, these requests have been determined in large part by the level of existing funding plus incremental increases. Submission of departmental requests to the Budget Division takes place two to three months prior to the opening of the legislative session.

Larger departments contain their own budget offices which may impose additional requirements in support of spending requests from their subdivisions. Frequently, the Budget Division indicates a need for such supporting documents to be submitted along with the budget requests. Within the various departments, different approaches are employed in arriving at spending estimates for the subdivisions. In some cases, strong indications of what each unit is expected to request are based on top-level department decisions. In others, these estimates are arrived at through consultations between higher-level and middle-management officials in each of the bureaus or divisions of the department. In still others, lower-level units submit estimates to departmental budget staff with relatively little restriction. Whatever system is used, however, the final decision as to the departmental budget requests rests with the head of each agency.

Once agency requests have been submitted to the Budget Division, that office then has the task of assembling all the data into a "tentative budget" to be presented to the governor. If any agency fails to submit a budget—no longer a problem—the governor may direct the preparation of estimates for that agency. The tentative budget includes proposed expenditures, by organization, from all state funds,

FIGURE 2
Executive Budget Preparation

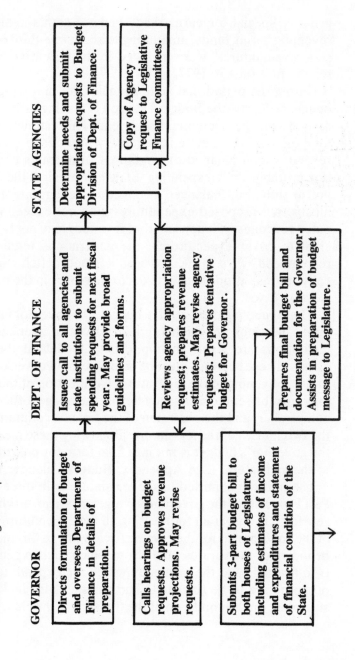

general, special, or earmarked. Federal grants-in-aid and revenue-sharing funds, amounting to about one-third of total state expenditures, were included in the executive budget for the first time in 1977.

During the period that state agencies are preparing their budget requests, the Budget Division is making estimates of revenue for the upcoming fiscal year. This estimate of the total income of the state is necessary in order to reconcile revenues with planned expenditures. Alabama's constitution prohibits deficit spending. State law requires the governor to submit a "balanced" budget to the legislature. This means that proposed expenditures may not exceed anticipated revenues. If it appears that revenues may not be sufficient to cover expenditures, the governor is required to recommend ways to meet the anticipated deficit. Specifically, he may propose new taxes or increases in the rates of existing taxes.

After receiving the tentative budget, the governor initiates public hearings at which representatives of agencies and institutions are given an opportunity to defend their requests. These hearings must be held at least two weeks prior to the convening of the legislature. Notification of the hearings must be sent to all agency heads, the budget officer, the comptroller, and the chairmen of the finance committees of the two houses of the legislature. Following these meetings, the governor's budget is put into final form for presentation to the legislature. (See Appendix, Budget Calendar.)

The budget submitted to the legislature is in three parts. Part I consists of the governor's budget message, in which he sets forth his program for meeting all the expenditure needs of the government for the coming fiscal year. In this message he indicates the various funds from which each expenditure is to be made and the means by which the expenditures he proposes are to be financed. The message also includes a statement on the condition of the treasury at the close of the previous fiscal year, on the estimated condition of the treasury at the end of the fiscal year then in progress, and on the estimated condition of the treasury at the end of the fiscal year covered by the budget. The state's revenue and debt situation are detailed and, if necessary, the governor sets forth his plan for meeting any anticipated deficit.

Part II contains the detailed breakdown of proposed expenditures by organizational unit, noting the funds from which each of the expenditures are to be made. This part of the document provides a basis for comparison by listing the actual expenditures for each purpose by each organization for the two most recently completed fiscal years. It also displays the estimated expenditures for the current fiscal year along with the amounts requested by each spending unit for the upcoming fiscal period. Finally, the governor's recommended appropriations are set forth. Part III of the budget consists of proposed appropriation and revenue bills for carrying into effect the governor's recommendations.

Legislative Authorization

One of the principles of American democracy insists that the "power of the purse" be vested in the legislative branch of government. This means, in practice, that no money may be spent from the public treasury except those amounts authorized by the legislature. Alabama's constitution is specific on this point: "No money shall be paid out of the treasury except upon appropriations made by law."[2] In addition, this power of appropriation may not be delegated by the legislature to any other official or body.[3]

The budget presented to the legislature is the governor's plan for financing state government. The legislature is responsible for examining this plan and has the legal authority to modify it in any way, either increasing or reducing the governor's requests. In practice, the tradition of gubernatorial domination of the legislature has meant that significant

FIGURE 3
Legislative Branch Fiscal Organization

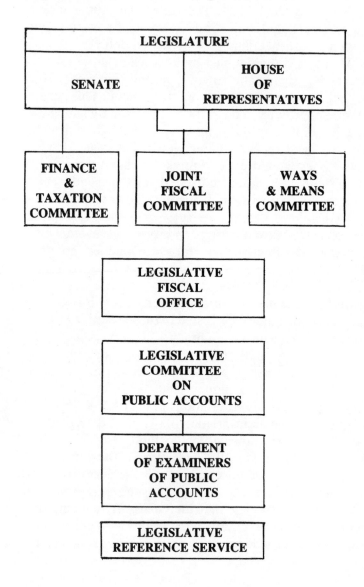

FIGURE 4
LEGISLATIVE AUTHORIZATION

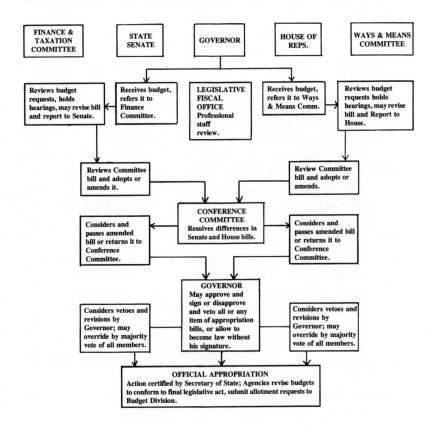

alterations of the executive budget seldom occur. It is normal practice, however, for some relatively minor increases
or decreases, additions or deletions, to be made by the
legislature.

When the governor's budget is received, the legislature's
review mechanism goes into operation. The document is
sent to the standing committees in each house with responsibility for recommending appropriations. These committees
are Ways and Means in the House of Representatives and
Finance and Taxation in the Senate. Although not required,
it has been customary for these two committees to hold joint
hearings in advance of the regular session. Representatives
of state agencies and institutions are invited to appear and
present justifications for their spending requests. This gives
members of the key legislative committees an opportunity to
examine the budget requests—the same figures presented to
the Budget Division—before actually receiving the governor's budget. It also reduces the number and scope of hearings required after the formal budget document is received.
It is customary, however, for members of the joint committee to avoid making public commitments on agency requests
prior to submission of the governor's budget.

Any revisions made by the two legislative committees are
subsequently incorporated into the appropriation bills reported out to each house. The legislature does not enact the
budget as a single document. Rather, it translates the budget
into law through the passage of several appropriation acts.
At each regular session, two major appropriation bills are
enacted: first, the general appropriation act and, second, the
educational appropriation act, which distributes revenues in
the Special Educational Trust Fund. In addition, numerous
special appropriation acts are usually passed. These bills are
subject to the same procedures governing other legislation.
This means that appropriation bills require three readings
before passage, that they are subject to change by the ap-

propriations committees in both houses, and that they may be debated and amended from the floor prior to enactment. Like other bills, appropriation acts must pass both houses in identical form and be signed by the governor before becoming law.

The governor of Alabama possesses the item veto power. That is, he may strike out any item in an omnibus appropriation act without having to veto the entire bill, thus allowing the remainder of the measure to become law. The legislature, of course, may override an item veto in the same manner as a regular executive veto, by a majority vote of the total membership of both houses.

What is not clear, however, is whether the governor may line-item veto a portion of an appropriation bill after the legislature has adjourned. As of this writing, there is no record of such action ever having been taken, although the question arose in 1976 when the governor indicated he might "pocket-veto" selected items in the General Fund appropriations bill. No such action was taken, however, and a possible court test of the power was avoided.

In addition, the governor possesses the power of executive amendment of appropriation bills. This, indeed, seems to have been the principal means by which chief executives have altered legislative money bills. In this way, the governor may return an appropriation bill to the legislature with suggested modifications, avoiding the necessity to sign or veto the measure as it stands. An executive amendment is subject to being overridden by a majority of the elected membership of both houses. However, if accepted by both houses, it is then incorporated into the act and sent back to the governor for his signature. One survey of the use of this device, covering the period 1903–1947, found that only 7 of 235 executive amendments were rejected by the Alabama legislature.[4] A more recent examination of the period 1949–1973, dealing with appropriation bills only, found 8 of 9 executive amendments were accepted.[5] During the same period, not a single use of the item veto could be found. It appears, therefore, that Alabama governors have been inclined to deal with legislative budget actions almost exclusively through the executive-amendment procedure.

In keeping with the prohibition against deficit spending, funds are appropriated as "maximum conditional and proportionate appropriations." In other words, the funds are approved subject to revenues being available to cover the appropriated amounts. Should anticipated revenue fail to materialize during the course of the fiscal year, the governor is authorized to reduce allotments, but only for all agencies proportionate to the percent of the revenue deficit. In addition, the general appropriation bill contains an emergency appropriation not to exceed 2 percent of the total. This emergency reserve may be allotted by the governor for any legal purpose for which no appropriation was made or for which the regular appropriation proved insufficient. In 1977, the Alabama House adopted a rule requiring that a $4 million surplus be provided in the General Fund for the 1978/79 fiscal year.

The legislature, meeting infrequently and possessing little staff assistance, has found itself at a disadvantage in dealing with the budget. For the most part, legislators have been dependent upon information gathered by executive-branch agencies in arriving at spending decisions. In an effort to provide itself with the internal ability to gather and analyze budgetary data, the legislature in 1973 created the position of "fiscal consultant." This individual and his assistant were appointed by the chairmen of the House Ways and Means and Senate Finance and Taxation committees and reported to those committees. In 1975, the consultant approach was modified through the creation of the Legislative Fiscal Office mentioned in chapter two. In addition, this action also established a continuing legislative committee known as the Joint Fiscal Committee. The committee, which includes members from the two appropriating committees plus the lieutenant governor and the Speaker of the House, is responsible for overseeing the work of the director and staff of the Legislative Fiscal Office.

The new fiscal office was empowered to obtain necessary information relating to expenditures from all the departments, agencies, and institutions of state government. In addition, the staff has access to all information compiled by the Legislative Reference Service and the Department of Examiners of Public Accounts, although independent of both those long-established agencies. The function of the Legislative Fiscal Office is to provide to the House Ways and Means and Senate Finance and Taxation committees "information which will assist such committees in the discharge of all matters within their jurisdictions, including:

(1) information with respect to the budget, appropriation bills, and other bills authorizing or providing budget authority or tax expenditures;

(2) information with respect to revenues, receipts, estimated future revenues and receipts, and changing revenue conditions; and

(3) such related information as such committees may request."[6]

The act creating the Legislative Fiscal Office also authorized "up-to-date" computer technology and the employment of staff trained in its use. In short, the legislature took a long step toward correcting its traditional weakness in the area of budgetary information and analysis. Fully staffed and funded, the Legislative Fiscal Office could rival the Budget Division in expertise.

Budget Execution

Following appropriation of funds by the legislature, responsibility for implementation and control of the budget reverts to the executive branch. Control is the dominant characteristic of the budget process. In part, this emphasis can be traced to the origins of budgeting as part of the reformist reaction against corruption in government. In Alabama, a control emphasis is furthered by the requirement for a balanced budget. The principal method by which control is exerted is through the allotment process. In addition, the Department of Finance imposes some control over agency spending through the requirement that the department approve all purchase orders and travel vouchers. The comptroller exercises the preaudit responsibility through which he determines the correctness and legality of every claim and account submitted for payment. At the same time, he assures that the necessary funds have been appropriated and alloted, and that there is sufficient money in the treasury for payment.

Allotment. The allotment procedure, however, is at the heart of budget execution. After money has been appropriated by the legislature, state law requires that it be apportioned to the spending organizations on a periodic basis—not to exceed three months—throughout the fiscal year.[7] This is one of the principal tasks of the Budget Division. No expenditure can be made without such an allotment. Although the allotment period may be determined by the Department of Finance, the usual practice is to make funds available to spending units on a quarterly basis, effective on the first day of October, January, April, and July. Agency requests for allotments must be made at least twenty days before the expiration of the current allotment.

Quarterly allotments do not have to be in equal portions. That is, not all agencies will receive 25 percent of their annual appropriation at the beginning of each quarterly period. Some agencies have special seasonal needs or program start-up costs that might require a larger than normal distribution during a particular quarter. Modification of the allotments may be made at any time by the Department of Finance, subject to the governor's approval. Requests for changing allotments usually are initiated by the agency head or the director of finance. It should be kept in mind that the purpose of the allotment procedure is to insure that spending agencies plan their activities in such a way as to avoid deficiencies which might force curtailment of operations later in the fiscal year.

The use of the allotment system as a control on agency expenditures is weakened by the exemption of capital projects, certain special funds, and some federal grants. In practice, this omits a substantial portion of total state funds from the allotment process. In addition, there is some evidence that allotments may not always prevent agency overspending. In mid-1977, for example, the attorney general's office sought a supplemental appropriation of more than $300,000 to cover an anticipated shortfall in available funds. The action resulted in disclosure that quarterly allotments had greatly exceeded the amounts which normally would have been available for the first two quarters of the fiscal year.[8] At that point, the agency already had been allotted more than 90 percent of its General Fund appropriation for the entire year. A reduction in anticipated federal funds apparently accounted for the overdrawing against General Fund appropriations. However, a spokesman for the comptroller's office said "it would be very hard to tell" whether the allotments included federal funds or consisted wholly of General Fund money.[9]

Proration. Alabama's budget law provides for the prorationing of appropriations in the event it appears that there will be a deficiency in a state fund. Prorationing is a reduction in allotments (spending authority) in which all agencies or institutions drawing on a fund are reduced on a proportional basis. This may occur if, during the course of a fiscal year, it becomes apparent that revenues coming into a fund will fall short of the appropriations authorized from the fund. If, for example, the shortfall is perceived as 5 percent, then all spending units utilizing that fund would be reduced by 5 percent in authorized expenditures from the affected fund. This is a simplification of a complicated procedure that has been the object of much litigation over the years.

Supplemental Appropriations. Although the state's budget law provides for supplemental spending requests by the governor and, by implication, executive departments, it is a device seldom employed. In practice, agencies seeking supplemental appropriations during the course of a fiscal year, take such requests directly to the legislature. If approved, they are enacted as special legislation. The Budget Division becomes involved at two stages in the process: first, it must verify the availability of funds to cover the supplemental appropriation; secondly, such appropriations, like all others, are subject to the quarterly allotment process conducted by the central budget office.

Reversion. Finally, funds alloted to state agencies, but not spent or obligated by them during the fiscal year, revert to the treasury, specifically to the fund from which they were drawn. It has been customary for both the General Fund and the Special Educational Trust Fund to show surpluses at the end of the year. However, it has been unusual for agencies to revert funds that have been alloted to them during the year. When, in 1976, the Alabama Development Office returned $500,000 in unspent appropriations to the General Fund, it was hailed as "a first" in state history.

The Audit

Basically, the effort to control expenditures of public funds takes two forms. First, there are administrative controls such as allotment and prorationing, mentioned above. This category also includes periodic reporting by spending units to the central budget office and control by that office over transfers of funds from one purpose to another. In Alabama, such transfers can be accomplished only with the approval of the director of finance and the governor. A second form of control is "financial" control and relates to the accounting system established to document and record all expenditures. This latter category includes the audit function.

Auditing takes place at two points in time. That form of the procedure which occurs during the fiscal period for which spending has been authorized is called the preaudit. As previously mentioned, this action involves making certain that proposed expenditures are legitimate and that funds are available to cover the obligation. In Alabama, formal responsibility for the preaudit function is placed in the comptroller, an official within the Department of Finance. Clearance is required before spending can take place; thus preauditing is a part of budget execution and an important means of executive control.

The postaudit represents the final phase of the budget process. It normally takes place after the end of the fiscal year and is conducted by officers and agencies outside the executive branch. It serves to ensure that all spending has taken place in accordance with the legal intent of the legislature and that the accounting figures maintained by spending agencies are accurate. It is, in other words, concerned with both the legality of transactions and the accuracy of accounts. The auditing agency usually reports its findings directly to the legislature.

Preauditing and postauditing serve different purposes. Preauditing is essentially an administrative tool to determine the legality of expenditures before they are made and is conducted within the executive branch. The postaudit, on the other hand, is concerned primarily with verifying the financial transactions of the administration, attesting to the accuracy and fairness of the administration's representations, and reporting its findings to the legislative branch.[10]

In Alabama, the principal auditing agency is the Department of Examiners of Public Accounts, created by the legislature in 1947. There is, however, a certain duality in regard to this function owing to the existence of the constitutionally created and independently elected office of the state auditor.

The Auditor. The office of state auditor was created by the state constitution in 1901. That charter, however, left the duties of this official unclear beyond stating that he "shall perform such duties as may be required by law" and that the auditor and treasurer shall annually "make a full and complete report to the governor, showing the receipts and disbursements of every character, all claims audited and paid out, by items, and all taxes and revenues collected and paid into the treasury, and the sources thereof."[11]

Although a constitutional officer, popularly elected to a four-year term, the principal functions of the auditor are based on legislative action. The basic grant of authority, enacted in 1939, requires the auditor to postaudit the accounts and records of the Department of Finance and the state treasurer.[12] In recent years, the office has extended its auditing functions to other state agencies and to the accounts of some cities and counties. This procedure has been defended on the ground that the language in the state constitution is not limiting and that the records of the Department of Finance include transactions of virtually every unit of government within the state.

Examiners of Public Accounts. In spite of the existence of a constitutionally created office of state auditor, the principal auditing agency in Alabama is the Department of Examiners of Public Accounts. Created by act of the legislature in 1947, this office is headed by a chief examiner who is appointed by and is responsible to the Legislative Committee on Public Accounts. He serves a seven-year term and may be reappointed indefinitely. The joint legislative committee which oversees the work of the examiners was created specifically for that purpose and reflects the general principle that the postaudit is a responsibility of the legislature. Membership on the committee consists of the president of the Senate, the Speaker of the House of Representatives, and five members from each of the two houses of the legislature. The Senate president serves as committee chairman and the Speaker as vice-chairman.[13]

With a staff of more than a hundred, the department is required to audit the books of every state and county agency at least once every two years. Municipalities and city boards of education may be audited at their request. In the case of cities and towns, the cost of the audit is borne by the local government.

During 1974, aided by a $50,000 revenue-sharing grant, the department established a new Operational Audits Division to conduct a limited number of "performance audits." This approach puts greater emphasis on how well an agency of government is doing its job, not just whether its books are balanced. It extends the auditing function beyond the determination of legality of expenditures into the broader areas of managerial efficiency and program effectiveness. In short, a performance audit tries to determine whether an agency has carried out its programs in such a way as to achieve the objectives set by the legislature.

The postaudit concludes the budgeting cycle. The audit reports, submitted to the legislature, provide a basis for future policy decisions. In addition, they serve to call to the attention of agency officials possible deficiencies in program administration and prompt corrective actions to prevent similar mistakes in the future.

Summary

In Alabama, then, as in more than forty other states, the

principal responsibility for preparing the budget rests with the governor. To be more exact, it rests with a professional staff directly responsible to the governor. The state budget officer is an official in the Department of Finance, appointed by the director of that department with the approval of the governor.

The budget process begins when operating agencies and institutions are asked to submit their spending estimates to the Budget Division. Although it has been customary to issue certain general instructions to the agencies, the Budget Division has not normally imposed fixed ceilings on agency requests. Rather, each unit preparing a budget request has been relatively free to submit estimates based on its view of the funding necessary to carry out its responsibilities during the next fiscal period.

Agency budgets are submitted simultaneously to the Budget Division and to the legislature's finance committees. The latter normally undertake joint public hearings prior to the convening of the entire legislature. Executive budget hearings are conducted at the call of the governor. In practice, the legislature has not taken action on budget requests until after receipt of the governor's budget which usually contains substantial adjustments in agency spending requests. Consideration of appropriation bills is one of the most time-consuming and frequently controversial activities of the legislature. In the past, final resolution of budget bills has been among the last matters to be concluded prior to adjournment.

The extensive practice of earmarking revenues and a heavy dependence upon federal grants and revenue sharing have combined to place a major portion of total expenditures outside the normal budgetary-review process. With perhaps as much as 90 percent of all revenues set aside for predetermined uses, the discretionary authority of both the governor and the legislature is restricted. A result is that program needs and available revenues are not always balanced. The constitutional requirement of a "balanced" budget, while not preventing deficit financing through borrowing, has made it difficult for state policy makers to institute new programs without, at the same time, finding new sources of revenue.

Once the legislature has approved appropriations bills, three basic practices are instituted to control spending by state agencies and institutions. First, most units of government receive funds via a quarterly allotment process. Second, the state comptroller—and, in some cases, the agencies themselves—impose a preaudit requirement to insure that all spendings requests are legitimate and that funds to cover the outlay are available. Finally, all expenditures are subject to a postaudit by the Department of Examiners of Public Accounts, a legislative agency whose findings are reported directly to the legislature. In addition, the financial records of the state treasurer and the Department of Finance are subject to examination by the state auditor.

4

Revenue and Expenditure Trends

Budgeting is basically a plan for spending money. But expenditures are inextricably linked to revenues. This is particularly the case in states like Alabama where the constitution requires a "balanced" budget. Income, in other words, must be equal to outgo in any given fiscal period. State law obligates the governor to recommend new or increased revenue sources in the event anticipated expenditures appear likely to exceed forecast income. It should be noted, however, that taxes and expenditures do not balance neatly. This is because both revenue estimating and expenditure forecasting are inexact sciences. In addition, less than one-half of all state revenues are derived from taxes. The remainder comes from such sources as ABC (liquor)-store profits, federal funds, payments into state employees' and teachers' retirement systems, and a variety of less substantial items such as fees, rents, fines, and the like.

Sources of Revenue

For most purposes, state income can be divided into two categories: tax and nontax sources. During the 1975 fiscal year, Alabama obtained 49.7 percent of its revenues from tax sources and 50.3 percent from nontax sources. Table 1 indicates the breakdown by major sources in each category.

Nontax sources. The single largest source of nontax revenue received by the state is in the form of federal aid. Grants

TABLE 1
ALABAMA REVENUE SOURCES 1974–75

Source	Amount	Percent
TAXES		
General Sales & Use Tax	$354,750,942	15.67
Income Tax	242,607,415	10.71
Gasoline Tax	131,751,481	5.82
Tobacco Tax	46,199,407	2.04
Utilities Tax (Gross Receipts)	47,396,506	2.09
Alcohol Beverage Control Board	44,838,841	1.98
Insurance Companies (fees and gross-premium license)	35,849,469	1.58
Motor Vehicle License	33,670,656	1.49
Corporation (Franchise, etc.)	29,241,081	1.29
State Beer Tax & County License	27,807,225	1.23
General Property	27,934,721	1.23
All Other Taxes	104,261,639	4.61
NONTAX RECEIPTS		
Federal Funds (Grants & Revenue Sharing)	608,575,066	26.88
Teachers' Retirement System	274,337,123	12.12
State Employees' Retirement System	165,052,926	7.29
Other Nontax	90,108,698	3.97
TOTAL RECEIPTS	$2,264,383,196	100.00

*Source: State of Alabama, Department of Finance, *Annual Report,* Fiscal Year 1975.

for highways, schools, welfare, and numerous other functions of government exceeded $608 million in fiscal 1975. This consisted of approximately $544 million in categorical grants and $64 million in revenue-sharing funds. All federal aid amounted to nearly 27 percent of state revenues and was equal to roughly 54 percent of total state tax receipts, exceeding the amount collected from the state sales and income taxes combined. As has been the case for the past twenty years, federal aid constituted the single largest source of state income. The principal recipients of this aid, by program category, were (1) education: $144 million; (2) health, including mental health: $142 million, and (3) highways: $101 million.[1]

In addition to federal aid, the largest nontax contributions consisted of payments into the Teacher's Retirement System and the State Employees' Retirement System which accounted for nearly 20 percent of all receipts in 1975. Although normally classified as a nontax source, ABC-store profits of some $44 million have, in recent years, been classified as tax receipts in the compilations of the Department of Finance. However classified, this figure represents less than 2 percent of total state revenue.

Tax sources. Although only about one-half of the state's receipts are in the form of taxes, it is this category which most interests a majority of citizens and which provokes the greatest amount of political debate. According to the U.S. Census Bureau, Alabamians in 1972 paid an average of $232.95 per person in state taxes. While somewhat below the national average of $288.35, the figure represented an increase of 71 percent since 1967.

The state relies on some forty tax sources, most of which produce insignificant amounts of revenue. Like most states, Alabama derives the bulk of its tax receipts from three basic taxes: the general sales and use tax, the income tax, and the motor-fuels (gasoline) tax. These three accounted for more than 60 percent of state tax revenues in 1975 and produced more than 30 percent of income from all sources. In addition, taxes on tobacco products, public utilities, insurance companies, corporations, and the general property levy contributed substantial amounts of revenue, as shown in Table 1.

Each of these major sources of tax revenue will be discussed briefly in the pages that follow.[2]

Sales and Use Tax. The single most productive tax imposed by the state is that on general sales, levied at a 4 percent rate. A similar tax is placed on merchandise purchased outside the state and brought into Alabama. Net receipts from this tax in 1975 amounted to $354,750,942, or 15.67 percent of the revenue dollar. This tax is applied to most consumer purchases, including food and medicine. Some services, such as laundry and dry cleaning, barbering, and doctor and dentist fees, are exempt. In addition, a lower rate of 1.5 percent is placed on automobile sales. Approximately 90 percent of the sales tax and all of the use tax is earmarked for the Special Educational Trust Fund.

Income Tax. In Alabama, as in most states, the income tax is applied to both individual and corporate earnings. Second only to the sales tax in productivity, personal and corporate income taxes totaled $242,607,415 in the 1974/75 fiscal year, or 10.71 percent of revenues. Although lumped together for reporting purposes, the state normally derives about two and one-half times as much revenue from the personal income tax as from the corporate income tax. The individual income tax applies to residents of the state and to nonresidents who earn income within Alabama. The applicable rate in both instances ranges from 1.5 percent on amounts up to and including $1,000 of taxable income to a maximum of 5 percent on amounts in excess of $5,000. The corporate income tax is a flat 5 percent applied to domestic corporations as well as out-of-state firms doing business in Alabama. In the latter case, only earnings within the state are subject to the tax. Except for a small amount ($6.2 million in 1975) set aside for property-tax relief, proceeds from the income tax are earmarked by law for the Special Educational Trust Fund.

Gasoline Tax. Like every other state, Alabama imposes a tax on purchases of gasoline. The seven cents per gallon rate produced $131,751,481 in 1975, equal to 5.82 percent of all revenues. A separate tax of eight cents per gallon on diesel fuel added $14,443,425 to the state's income. Approximately $32 million of the gasoline revenue was used to service the bonded indebtedness of the Highway Department. Some $70 million was distributed to counties ($63 million) and municipalities ($7 million) for road construction and maintenance, and most of the remainder was earmarked for highways.

Tobacco Tax. Historically, state governments imposed taxes on the sale of specific items such as gasoline, liquor, and tobacco before they adopted general sales taxes. In Alabama, tobacco in virtually all its forms is subject to a variety of state taxes, ranging from twelve cents per pack of cigarettes to one-tenth of a cent on small cigars. Combined, these taxes contributed more than $46 million in 1975, nearly half of which was earmarked for education. Approximately 10 percent of these revenues ($4.3 million) was set aside by law for mental-health programs. An additional $3.7 million went to the Department of Pensions and Security (welfare), while more than $7 million wound up in the General Fund. Although receipts from the tobacco tax have doubled during the past ten years, they still account for only 2 percent of total state revenues.

Property tax. Real property in Alabama is assessed for tax purposes at varying rates not to exceed 30 percent of its "fair and reasonable" market value. Primarily a local government tax, the state rate is only 6.5 mills ($6.50 per $1,000 assessed value.) With property throughout the state assessed at approximately one-fifth its real market value, the effective rate is one of the lowest in the nation. Only Alaska, among all the states, derives a smaller percentage of total state and local tax collections from this source. In 1975, the property tax produced just under $28 million for state government in Alabama, about 1.25 percent of total revenues. It should be kept in mind, however, that five out of every six dollars paid in property taxes by Alabamians goes to local governments, most of it for the support of local school systems.

In June, 1972, Amendment 325 was added to the Alabama constitution providing that for *state* property-tax purposes utility properties were to be assessed at 30 percent of "fair and reasonable market values"; agricultural, forest, and residential properties at 15 percent, and all other property at 25 percent of fair and reasonable market value. Consistent with provisions in the amendment, the legislature also ordered statewide property reappraisal, on a county-by-county basis. The role of property taxes in the state's tax structure has declined sharply from approximately 50 percent of all taxes in 1915 to only 2.5 percent in 1975. Thus, changes brought about by the reappraisal program were expected to have only a slight effect on overall state revenues.

Motor Vehicle Licenses. Reflecting the increased presence of the automobile as well as a quadrupling of the basic fee, receipts from the sale of automobile, truck, and bus licenses have shown phenomenal growth in Alabama. Income from this source rose from $2.2 million in 1955 to $33.6 million just twenty years later. The tax, imposed on all types of motor vehicles, ranges from $7 a year for motorcycles to $13 for automobiles and a maximum of $780 on large trucks. In addition, the state received $5.4 million in 1975 from drivers license charges. In spite of the marked increase in recent years, Alabama derives less than 4 percent of total tax income from these sources, ranking forty-sixth among all the states. In 1975, about 87 percent of motor vehicle-license taxes went to the Highway Department. Most of the remainder, after administrative costs were deducted, was apportioned among the counties and municipalities of the state for use in construction and maintenance of public highways and streets. All receipts from driver's license fees are assigned to the General Fund.

Other Taxes. In addition to the major tax sources discussed above, Alabama utilizes more than thirty other kinds of levies, only a few of which are highly productive. Among these are the corporation franchise tax, the beer tax, the tax on gross receipts of public utilities, and a privilege license tax on insurance companies. The leading revenue producer among these is the 4 percent tax on gross receipts of utilities operating in the state. This tax, earmarked for education, contributed more than $47 million in 1975. Insurance companies doing business in the state are charged an annual fee plus a tax based on premiums collected. These revenues, almost $36 million in 1975, constitute the single largest source of income for the General Fund. About 80 percent of the amount collected, or some $28.5 million, went into the General Fund with the remainder divided between education and health funds. A state tax of five cents on each twelve fluid ounces of beer plus a state and county beer license fee produced $27.8 million in 1975. After deducting administrative costs and returning $2.7 million to county governments, the remainder was divided among the Special Educational Trust Fund ($11 million), the Department of Pensions and Security ($5.5 million), and the General Fund ($7.8 million).

Revenue Trends

Alabama's revenue sources, as shown in Figure 5, have undergone some modification over the past two decades in terms of their relative importance. Throughout the period, federal-aid funds have constituted the principal source of income for state government. For most of this period, the general sales tax has been the second most productive source. However, the percentage of state income derived from the sales tax has declined steadily since 1964 and in the most recent period has been surpassed by contributions and earnings of the two principal retirement systems (teachers and state employees). Dramatic increases in contributions to these two systems resulted from legislative actions in 1973 and 1975 expanding membership in the retirement programs and greatly increasing benefits. By way of illustration, total

FIGURE 5
Major Revenue Sources 1956-1975

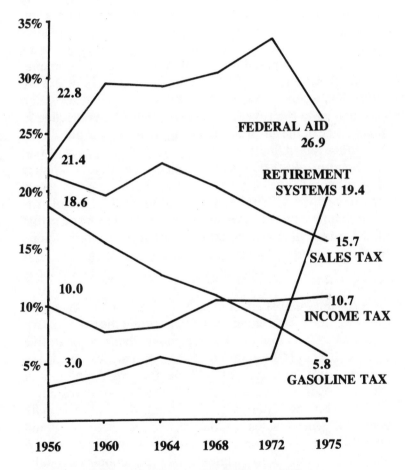

*Source: State of Alabama, Department of Finance,
Annual Report, Fiscal Years 1956-1975.

contributions to the Teachers' Retirement System in 1956 amounted to just $6.6 million. By 1972 this had climbed to $40.6 million. But in 1975, contributions and earnings accruing to the program surpassed $274 million.

Both federal-aid funds and contributions to retirement systems are classed as nontax sources of revenue. The amounts attributed to these two categories helps to explain the shift toward a greater emphasis on nontax revenues within the state's fiscal structure. Twenty years ago, taxes accounted for 67 percent of all state revenues in Alabama. As noted earlier, today's breakdown is just about evenly divided between tax and nontax sources. A final observation with regard to the revenue picture is the relative decline in importance of the gasoline tax throughout this period. This is due not to any reduction in the tax rate or lessening of fuel consumption. Rather, it simply reflects the greater reliance upon other revenue sources. Actually, gasoline taxes generated more than $131 million in 1975, more than double the $60 million produced by this source in 1956. The point is that all the principal revenue sources produce far more income for the state today than they did ten or twenty years ago. It is only the *relative* contribution of each source that has changed.

Of related interest is a comparison of Alabama's tax structure with that of its immediate neighbors and the averages for all states in the country. Table 2 shows these comparative figures. It should be noted that the percentages are of tax revenue only and do not include income from nontax sources. Although no startling differences are revealed, it can be seen that Alabama relies somewhat more heavily upon the general sales tax than is the case nationally and underutilizes the income tax. However, when compared with its five neighboring states, Alabama occupies a middle point between the national and regional averages with regard to these two tax sources. A larger portion of Alabama's tax revenue is derived from the so-called excise taxes (motor fuels, alcoholic beverages, and tobacco) than is the case either nationally or regionally. Sales and excise taxes, because they usually are applied at flat rates, are generally regarded as regressive. That is, they impose a relatively heavier burden on persons with lower incomes than on those in higher earnings brackets. To the extent that this is true, Alabama's tax structure would have to be classified as more regressive than that of the average American state. On the other hand, it would appear to be less regressive (or more progressive) than the composite tax system derived from combining and averaging tax sources of the five neighboring states.

TABLE 2
COMPARISON OF TAX REVENUE, BY SOURCE: 1971

	Percentage Distribution					
	General Sales	Income[1]	Motor Fuels	Alcoholic Beverages	Tobacco	Motor Vehicles
United States	30.0	26.3	12.9	3.0	4.9	6.2
ALABAMA	32.5	17.8	17.4	6.3	5.4	3.8
Five Southeast[2]	37.7	15.4	16.5	4.7	4.8	5.4

[1]Individual and corporate income taxes combined.
[2]Florida, Georgia, Louisiana, Mississippi, Tennessee (averaged)
*Source: Advisory Commission on Intergovernmental Relations, *Federal–State–Local Finances,* 1973–1974 edition.

Revenue Effort

State governments differ in their ability to raise revenues and make differing levels of effort in utilizing the revenue capacity they possess. Since taxes must be paid out of the income stream, states ranking near the bottom in per capita income—Alabama is one of these—generally are regarded as possessing a more limited revenue capability than those in which personal incomes are higher. The critical question, then, is to what extent does a given state make use of its revenue-raising capacity? One further refinement is necessary in approaching this question. This has to do with the degree of centralization or decentralization built into the state's revenue system. In brief, some states—again, Alabama is an example—have highly centralized revenue structures in which the bulk of combined state and local revenues are collected by the state government. Other states—New Hampshire, New Jersey, and South Dakota, for instance—have decentralized systems in which a majority of revenues are collected by local units of government. In 1971, for example, state government collected 74 percent of all state and local taxes in Alabama. This compared with a national average of 54 percent. For this reason, comparisons of tax effort or, more broadly, revenue effort, usually combine state and local sources.

Table 3 provides a comparison of total revenue effort by Alabama with national and regional averages in the years 1965 and 1971. It indicates that Alabama made a slightly higher effort in 1965 than did the average state, but fell below the national mean in 1971. In the latter year, Alabama ranked twenty-eighth among the fifty states in revenue effort, that is, in the percentage of personal income paid in taxes and charges to state and local governments. The table also reveals that in both years Alabama made a substantially smaller revenue effort than did its neighbors, using average figures for the other five Deep South states. Although only Tennessee in this group made a lower effort in 1965, three of the five states—Florida, Georgia, and Tennessee—fell below Alabama in 1971. The regional average was heavily influenced by extraordinary revenue efforts on the part of Louisiana and Mississippi.

A 1976 tax-effort survey by the U. S. Department of

Commerce ranked Alabama forty-ninth among the fifty states. Combined state and local taxes in Alabama were $455.19 per capita, compared to an average for all the states of $730.52. Put another way, total state and local taxes in Alabama took just 9.9 percent of personal income, while nationally the figure was 12.5 percent. In part, these figures reflected the heavy reliance on nontax sources of revenue in Alabama.

TABLE 3
COMPARISON OF REVENUE EFFORT

	Revenues as Percent of Personal Income[1]		State Percent as Percent of U.S. Average	
	1971	1965	1971	1965
United States	14.9	12.8	100	100
ALABAMA	14.3	12.9	96	101
Five Southeast[2]	15.1	14.1	101	111

[1]Total state and local tax collections plus all charges and miscellaneous general revenue.
[2]Florida, Georgia, Louisiana, Mississippi, and Tennessee (averaged).
*Source: Advisory Commission on Intergovernmental Relations, *Federal–State–Local Finances,* 1973–1974 edition.

Expenditure Trends

Traditionally, the "big three" of state government expenditures have been education, highways, and public welfare. This has been the pattern of state outlays in Alabama until quite recently. During the past few years, expenditures on public health programs—largely concentrated in the Medicaid program providing health care assistance to the indigent—have surpassed spending for welfare. Were Medicaid costs assigned to the welfare category, this change of relative position would not have occurred. Table 4 shows

the breakdown of major categories of state spending during
the 1975 fiscal year. Although not shown in the table, the
impact of expanded retirement programs for state employees and teachers has been substantial. For example,
teachers'-retirement outlays for 1975 totalled almost $250
million, equal to about 25 percent of all educational expenditures. Similarly, state-employees' retirement costs exceeded $123 million, constituting more than one-half of total
expenditures in the category "Protection to Persons and
Property."

TABLE 4
ALABAMA EXPENDITURES, 1974–1975

Purpose	Amount	Percent
Education	$1,005,412,245	45.17
Highways	238,162,476	10.70
Health & Sanitation	206,099,813	9.26
Protection to Persons & Property (Law Enforcement, Business Regulation, Military, etc.)	202,330,752	9.09
Public Welfare	141,220,667	6.34
Debt Service	76,720,947	3.45
General Government (Executive Office, Legislature, Judiciary, Fiscal Administration, etc.)	75,975,897	3.41
Hospitals & Institutions for the Handicapped (including Department of Mental Health	58,191,167	2.62
Conservation & Natural Resources	34,474,596	1.55
All Other (Corrections, Recreation, payments to cities & counties, etc.)	187,298,668	8.41
TOTAL EXPENDITURES	$2,225,890,662	100.00

*Source: State of Alabama, Department of Finance, *Annual Report,* Fiscal Year
1975.

FIGURE 6
Expenditures, By Purpose, 1956-1975

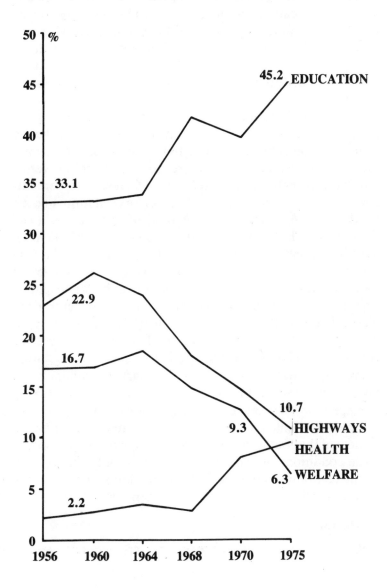

A pattern of major state expenditures in terms of their relative importance over the past twenty years is shown in Figure 6. Expressed as percentages of total outlays, it can be seen that education and highway expenditures have consistently ranked first and second throughout this period. Highway costs, however, as a share of the total, have declined somewhat in recent years, while educational expenditures have continued to consume a growing portion of the state dollar.

Looking at the four major areas of state expenditures from another angle, it can be seen that the state bears a heavy share of responsibility for these functions. Put another way, the Alabama expenditure picture, like the state's revenue structure, is highly centralized. Table 5 shows the percentage of total state and local government expenditures borne by the state for each of these broad program areas. (The figures exclude federal aid.) By comparison with national averages, it can be seen that state government in Alabama assumes a greater share of the financial burden for each of these functions, with the exception of health and hospitals. The state's expenditure distribution is also more centralized (state dominated) than that prevailing in the region as a whole. Only Louisiana, among the five states chosen for comparison, shows a stronger reliance upon state funding.

Previous studies have shown a marked tendency for lower-income states to rely more heavily upon state taxing and spending to finance shared functions. They have also revealed a definite pattern of state-dominated public finance in most of the southern states.[3] Since Alabama meets both of these conditions, it should not be surprising to find a more highly centralized revenue and expenditure structure in this state than throughout the nation, generally.

Indebtedness

When governmental revenues are insufficient to cover the

costs of planned programs and projects, the difference may be made up through borrowing. In recent years, especially in the period since World War II, Alabama, like most states, has borrowed heavily to finance capital expenditures. Most of this borrowing, done through the sale of the state's bonds, has been used to produce funds for highway-construction and school-building projects.

TABLE 5
PERCENTAGE OF STATE AND LOCAL GOVERNMENT EXPENDITURES, FROM OWN REVENUE SOURCES, FINANCED BY STATE GOVERNMENT, 1970–1971.

	Total General Expenditure	Local Schools	Highways	Public Welfare	Health & Hospitals
United States	52.7	43.3	74.5	76.1	51.5
ALABAMA	64.0	74.6	81.9	99.1	38.5
Five Southeast[1]	57.7	61.4	75.7	93.8	40.5

[1]Florida, Georgia, Louisiana, Mississippi, and Tennessee (averaged).
*Source: Advisory Commission on Intergovernmental Relations, *Federal–State– Local Finances,* 1973–1974 edition.

Although the state's constitution prohibits the incurring of "new debt," this provision, as noted in chapter 2, has been consistently ignored or circumvented throughout that document's seventy-five-year history. Some borrowing has been authorized by specific amendments to the constitution. Another method for legitimizing deficit financing has been to create public authorities for the purpose of selling securities, the proceeds of which are used to finance designated projects. Examples of this approach can be found in such agencies as the Alabama Building Finance Authority, the Alabama Pollution Control Finance Authority, the Corporation for Borrowing for Schools, and a half-dozen highway-finance authorities and commissions. All told, more than twenty such financing bodies exist.[4] Because such arrangements usually pledge specific revenues, such as a share of the gasoline tax or dormitory rentals, to the repayment of the principal and interest, the courts have generally held them not to violate the constitutional prohibitions against state debt.

Whatever may have been the intent of the authors of the state constitution, deficit financing of state-government operations through borrowing is a reality. In September, 1975, the state auditor announced that the bonded indebtedness of Alabama had passed the $1-billion mark for the first time in the state's history.[5] Servicing the debt, that is, paying the interest and principal due on it, cost the state more than $76 million in 1975. As shown in Figure 7, debt-service costs have nearly doubled in the past seven years.

Basically, there are two types of state debt. The first type, represented by general-obligation bonds, pledges the "full faith and credit" of the state, through its taxing power, to the repayment of the securities. Much greater use is made of the second type of debt instrument, so-called revenue bonds. In the latter case, the "full faith and credit" of the state is not pledged but anticipated revenues from the project are earmarked for payment of the principal and interest. Use of these "nonguaranteed" bonds constitutes the most important device for avoiding debt limitation. Because such bonds are not backed by the taxing power of the state, they generally carry interest charges about one-half of a percent higher than that imposed on general obligation bonds. The 1975 auditor's report showed that Alabama's bonded indebtedness consisted of approximately $895 million of revenue bonds, and $120 million general obligations, a ratio of better than seven to one in favor of the revenue-type security.

FIGURE 7
Debt Service Costs, 1956-1975

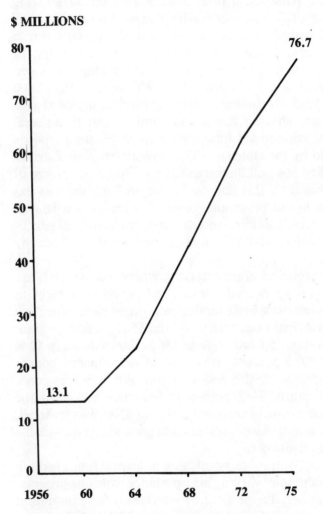

$ MILLIONS

*Source: State of Alabama, Department of Finance,
 Annual Report, Fiscal Years 1956-1975.

The Federal Influence

Before leaving the subject of trends in state revenue and expenditure patterns, a brief examination of the growing importance of federal-aid funding might be in order. As shown in Figure 5, this source has accounted for between 25 and 35 percent of the state's revenue in recent years. In terms of gross dollars, federal aid has steadily increased from approximately $74 million in 1956 to more than $600 million in 1975. Beginning in 1973, this source included general revenue-sharing funds that, unlike the traditional categorical grant-in-aid funds, were available for purposes determined by the state. In 1975, revenue-sharing distributions totalled $64 million or slightly more than 10 percent of all federal aid. Of this amount, some $8.5 million was expended on health programs, most of it for mental health; approximately $8 million went to support a variety of educational activities, and $6.5 million was used for highway projects.

In the categorical-grant category, where federal funds are used only for specifically designated purposes subject to conditions imposed by federal granting agencies, education was the principal beneficiary. Of the $544 million in grant money received by the state in 1975, approximately $144 million, or 26.5 percent, was used to help finance educational programs. Health and mental-health activities benefited from nearly $142 million in federal grants, and the Highway Department received just over $100 million. In all, nearly five hundred categorical grant programs are available to state governments.

The impact of this heavy infusion of federal funds is obviously considerable, varying in importance from one program area to another. In the field of education, for example, if payments to retired teachers and state contributions to Social Security are excluded, federal funds in 1975 accounted for about one dollar in every five of state expenditures. An even greater effect can be seen in funding highway programs, where 45 per cent of 1975 expenditures—almost one dollar in every two—came from federal-government grants. And in the area of public health, including mental health, almost three out of every four dollars spent by the state originated in a federal-grant or revenue-sharing fund. Similarly, about 70 percent of welfare outlays represented federal-aid dollars in 1975.

State policy makers and students of budgeting have been concerned about the impact of federal funds on state fiscal-policy decisions.[6] These concerns take several forms. First, there is the question of the extent to which state governments surrender control over program standards by accepting federal assistance. This is better understood as the so-called "guidelines" problem, in which certain conditions are attached to the use of the grant money. These conditions may range from setting wage scales for persons employed by the aided program to determining construction standards for a new highway. The effect is to transfer discretionary decision authority from the using agency to the federal counterpart responsibile for administering the grant program.

A second question related to the use of federal aid has to do with its effect on state budget priorities. It can be argued that the availability of federal grants in some program areas has led to shifts in the allocation of state funds away from unaided functions. Simply stated, if one dollar of state money will generate two dollars of federal funds in a particular program area, state policy makers are likely to appropriate for that program in preference to an activity for which federal funds are not available or are provided on a less favorable basis. An example would be the tendency of most states, including Alabama, to divert a greater portion of highway funds to the Interstate system, whose "matching" formula provides nine federal dollars for each state dollar.

Conversely, one might point to the corrections system, including principally the state's prisons where, until recently, no federal assistance was available, a fact that may help to account for the relative underfunding of this governmental function.

Finally, critics of state reliance upon federal-grant money point to the fact that much of this assistance goes to fund "pilot" programs, especially in the fields of education and health. Once these experimental programs have been established, the federal "seed money" may be withdrawn or reduced and the burden of continuing the program rests with the state. New sources of state revenue must be found or the programs must be curtailed.

Federal financial assistance to state governments has its positive aspects, as well. Not the least of these is the substantial addition to available state funds, thus enabling state governments to undertake many public service activities that most of them would find difficult to finance from their own resources. It also is a means by which state governments are encouraged to pursue important national goals. The availability of federal matching money serves as an incentive for states to participate more or less uniformly in such endeavors as upgrading the nation's highway system or improving the quality of public education and health care. In addition, the grant system enables the states to take advantage of the greater revenue-raising capacity of the federal government. With its dominance in the use of the income tax, the federal government is able to generate ever-increasing revenues as the economy expands and corporate and personal earnings increase. State tax systems, on the other hand, based largely on consumer taxes, are less "elastic," and in recent years the costs of state government have grown more rapidly than its revenues. Federal grants and revenue sharing return a portion of federal receipts to the states, reducing this disparity and compensating, to an extent, for the less-productive state tax systems.

Finally, federal grants provide a means of "equalizing" the level of public services among the various states. As noted earlier, the states have differing abilities to raise revenues from their own sources. Some states are relatively "rich," some are relatively "poor." Most federal grant programs are designed to distribute a greater portion of available funds to those states with less revenue raising capability, or make it less costly for the "poorer" states to share in the funding. Generally, this is done in one of two ways. First, the amount of federal money to be distributed may be apportioned among the states on the basis of a formula that makes more available, per capita, to states in which personal incomes are relatively low. A second approach is to adjust the matching formula in such a way as to require low-income states to contribute a smaller share of total state-federal funding for a given program. The purpose in both cases is to enable poorer states to offer certain services (health, education, etc.) at a level closer to that of the wealthier states than would otherwise be possible. As a result of these efforts, the budgets of poorer states generally include a larger portion of federal funds than do the budgets of wealthier states.

An examination of Alabama's revenue and expenditure data over the past two decades reveals certain definite trends. The most notable development, with regard to revenues, has been the shift toward greater reliance upon nontax sources. Slightly more than half of the state's income now comes from such sources, principally in the form of federal aid funds and contributions to the teachers' and state employees' retirement systems. Alabama's tax structure is not remarkably different from that found in most states. Sales, income, and gasoline taxes account for well over half of all tax revenues. Alabama's revenue picture, like that of most states in the south, is marked by a relatively high degree of centralization. That is, state government accounts for about three out of every four tax dollars collected by all units of government within the state.

Looking at expenditure trends over the same twenty-year period, the most visible developments have been the large increases in spending on education and the recent escalation in costs of servicing the state's mounting debt. Expenditures for education, highways, public health, and welfare have accounted for the bulk of state outlays throughout the period.

5

Problems and Prospects

How governments, at all levels, manage their financial affairs has become the subject of heightened public interest. This concern is attributable, in large part, to sharp increases in governmental activities—and costs—during the preceding two decades. During the period 1954–1974, all state and local taxes climbed from just $22 billion a year to over $138 billion, at which level they represented one out of every eight dollars of national income. State taxes alone increased more than 500 percent, nationally, during this period. And, despite a ten-fold increase in federal aid to state governments, total state debt expanded by 1,000 percent.

Alabama, its basic system of taxing and spending little changed for more than a quarter-century, has not escaped the clamor for "reform." Both the state's revenue structure and its procedures for allocating and spending funds have come under scrutiny. In this chapter, some of the principal criticisms or problems will be examined, along with a look at certain changes, both proposed and accomplished, aimed at improving the state's financial administration.

Regressive Taxes

Like most states, Alabama's revenue structure is heavily weighted in favor of consumer taxes. As noted in the preceding chapter, the general sales and use tax, along with levies on gasoline, tobacco, alcoholic beverages, and various license charges, account for the bulk of state tax revenues. These kinds of taxes are regarded as "regressive," in the sense that they impose a relatively greater burden on lower-income persons and families than on those with higher incomes. The sales tax, in particular, since it is applied to purchases of food and medicine, has been subjected to frequent criticism.

Most taxes, of course, have as their purpose—and their result—the transfer of resources from the private to the public sector. Without taxes and other sources of revenues, governments would find it impossible to provide the public goods and services that citizens demand. But different kinds of taxes distribute their burdens differentially throughout the population. Consumer-based levies—mainly sales and excise taxes—impact more forcefully upon lower-income persons and those with large families. Graduated income taxes, on the other hand, impose a greater burden upon middle- and upper-income groups. In Alabama, personal and corporate income taxes produce about 10 percent of all revenue and about 20 percent of all tax collections. All taxes tend to extract more from those who are relatively wealthy than from those who are classified as poor. It is the *percentage* of income required to pay taxes that determines whether a particular levy is "regressive" or "progressive."

The most frequently offered proposal for lightening the tax burden on lower-income persons without sacrificing state revenue has called for removing the sales tax on groceries and prescription drugs and making up the difference by either (a) extending the sales tax to services, such as haircuts and automobile repairs, now exempted, or (b) increasing the rates, scope, or both of the income tax. The head of the State Revenue Department's research division estimated that annual revenues could be increased by some $200 million by abolishing the sixty-four existing exemptions to the sales tax.[1] As for improving the productivity of the personal income tax, it has been suggested that the state's levy be tied directly to federal income-tax rates. Under this proposal, an individual would simply compute his federal tax, then add a fixed percentage—perhaps 15 or 20 percent—to be paid to the state.

Changes in the state's tax structure do not appear likely in the near future. Opposition to altering the sales tax is strong among professional education organizations because approximately 90 percent of the proceeds are earmarked for the Special Educational Trust Fund. In addition, the tax as now employed is the single most productive source of state tax revenue. The sales tax has the added appeal of being one levy that reaches virtually every citizen, thus ensuring that all contribute something to the costs of public services.

Although several states have adopted the federal income tax tie-in, others have shied away from such a connection. The principal drawback is the uncertainty introduced by linking state revenues to federal tax legislation. The fear is that a state could find its own tax collections reduced by a congressionally approved cut in the federal income tax, an action beyond the control of state policymakers. Proposals to increase corporate and personal income taxes also arouse opposition on grounds that such action would be detrimental to the state's industrial-development goals. Finally, opponents of an expanded income tax point to the heavy utilization of federal grants-in-aid and revenue sharing in the state's fiscal picture. Such funds, they point out, are derived primarily from collections of the progressive federal income-tax schedule, offsetting to some extent the regressivity of the state's revenue system.

State income-tax rates, in any event, are written into the state's constitution. Any attempt to extend the tax or increase the rates at which it is applied would require voter approval of a constitutional amendment. Such an effort was made in 1976 when a proposed amendment to increase the maximum personal income-tax rate from 5 to 6 percent was submitted to the legislature. The measure failed to receive the necessary legislative approval and was not placed on the ballot. A separate amendment to raise the maximum rate on the corporate income tax from 5 percent to 7.5 percent also failed to receive support in the legislature.

Earmarking

The ability of both the governor and the legislature to control state expenditures is seriously impaired by the extensive and traditional practice of earmarking revenues. The term refers to the channeling of certain revenues to specific programs either by statutory or constitutional provision. By setting aside such revenues for explicit and exclusive uses, they are effectively removed from the budgetary process, even though the amounts involved may be included in budget documents. In Alabama, this practice pervades financial administration. By 1976, about ninety cents of each state tax dollar had been pledged for a specific use. In short, the legislature has decided in advance that such monies may be used for a single designated purpose, and no other. Examples are the state sales tax, most of the proceeds of which go automatically into the Special Educational Trust Fund, and the gasoline tax, proceeds of which must be used exclusively for roads, streets, and highways. Some agencies of state government derive their entire budgets from earmarked revenues. The Department of Aeronautics, for example, is funded entirely by receipts from the state aviation-fuel tax.

In some instances, earmarking extends to broad purposes and the governor and legislature may exercise discretionary authority in distributing funds within the general program area. This is true of much of the money in the Special Educational Trust Fund. While this money can be used only for educational purposes, its distribution among various institutions, levels of education, and programs related to education, is subject to the decisions of elected policy makers. On the other hand, some earmarked revenues are more narrowly designated as to use. Most of the state income tax is pledged to the payment of teacher salaries and may not be used even for other educational purposes.

On at least two occasions, Alabama governors have attempted to reduce or eliminate earmarking of revenues. In 1945, Governor Chauncey Sparks succeeded in putting before the electorate a constitutional amendment "unearmarking" proceeds of the state income tax. Revenues from the income tax were originally set aside for property-tax reduction, a constitutional provision never implemented as a result of the failure to enact enabling legislation. Sparks sought to have the income-tax receipts placed in the state's general fund, but the proposal was overwhelmingly defeated. Later, an amendment was approved which earmarked the income-tax proceeds for teacher salaries.

In 1975, faced with a surplus in the Special Educational Trust Fund and shortages in the General Fund, Governor George C. Wallace backed a constitutional amendment that would have eliminated all earmarking and placed all state revenues in a single general fund. The proposed amendment failed to gain the necessary support in the legislature. A similar amendment failed to pass in the 1976 session.

The principal criticisms of earmarking revenues focus on its tendency to remove some public funds from regular scrutiny by elected officials and to inject a certain degree of rigidity into the state's financial affairs. Earmarking, especially where it is constitutionally prescribed, removes the designated revenues and expenditures from effective legislative control. More directly, it makes difficult or even impossible the transfer of public funds from program areas that may be over-financed to those that may be underfunded. In both 1975 and 1976, the Alabama legislature was engulfed in controversy as a result of efforts to divert funds from the Special Educational Trust Fund to programs operated by the Department of Mental Health.

Defenders of earmarking argue that it can be a means of linking benefits to taxes, as in the case of highways. By requiring gasoline and other motor vehicle taxes to be expended on highway construction and maintenance, only those who use the roads are directly taxed. In the language of economics, this represents a form of "indirect pricing." Interest groups that support certain governmental programs see earmarking as a way of assuring that such programs will have a steady, reliable source of revenue that is not subject to the shifting preferences of legislators and chief executives. Earmarking also has come about as a means of "selling" an unpopular tax by linking it with some needed or popular program such as education or mental health.[2] At bottom, however, earmarking reflects a lack of popular confidence in the legislature. The practice originated during a period in the nation's history when legislatures were distrusted as instruments of the public will. To the extent that such attitudes persist, efforts to eliminate the earmarking of revenues are not likely to succeed.

Legislative Reforms

The Alabama legislature, like its counterparts in most states, suffers severe handicaps in dealing with the budget. Not the least of these was the line-item format in which the budget data were presented prior to 1977. Lacking program description or evaluation of agency performance, such a budget was confined largely to itemizing the past and proposed outlays of governmental organizations and institutions. Confronted with thousands of entries no more descriptive than listings of amounts under headings such as "salaries," "supplies and materials," and "travel," even those members serving on the key finance committees had difficulty discerning the precise purposes for which the funds were requested. Legislative hearings, including those of the Joint Interim Committee on Finance and Taxation, provide an opportunity for questioning agency personnel about past performance and future plans. In the past, however, such hearings have been poorly attended and agency appearances frequently limited to less than thirty minutes. Coupled with such other disadvantages as lack of professional staff, relatively short and infrequent sessions, and the burden of dealing with large volumes of nonbudgetary legislation, even the most conscientious legislator has found it difficult to become well-informed on the complexities of budgeting. To a considerable extent, the legislature has been dependent upon information and analyses presented by the executive-branch agencies and the State Budget Office.

Two steps were taken during the mid-1970s to improve the legislature's ability to deal effectively with the budget. First, in 1975 a constitutional amendment was approved by the state's voters providing for annual sessions of the legislature.[3] In the same year, the legislature reorganized its internal mechanisms for handling the budget by creating the Legislative Fiscal Office and establishing a Joint Fiscal Committee.

Prior to 1975, Alabama had been one of only eight states in which the Legislature did not meet annually. As noted earlier, biennial sessions meant that revenue and expenditure estimates had to be forecast, in effect, three years into the future. It also had meant that special sessions were frequently required to consider financial matters. Under the annual-sessions provision, the legislature was authorized to meet for thirty legislative days within a 105 calendar-day period. Advocates of the change argued that, among other things, annual sessions would speed up the legislative process, especially with regard to budgetary matters. Typically, the state's operating budgets had been among the last items approved by the legislature prior to adjournment and, in some cases, agreement on the budgets had not been reached at all. In 1975, for example, the regular session of the legislature expired without enactment of the education budget. In 1971, the state operated for fifty-three days without either a General Fund budget or education appropriations. In 1976 and 1977, the first sessions under the new arrangement, both budgets were approved prior to adjournment.

In addition to annual sessions, the legislature moved to provide itself with professionalal analysis and advice through creation of the Legislative Fiscal Office. This office, given broad powers to acquire fiscal information from all departments of state government, replaced the office of "fiscal consultant" to the legislature that had been established in 1973. Named as the first director of the fiscal office was James V. Jordan, who previously had served as director of the Budget Division in the Department of Finance. The director and his staff report to the Joint Fiscal Committee, also established in 1975, and made up of members of the two appropriating committees of the legislature plus the lieutenant governor and the Speaker of the House of Representatives. Both of these innovations, designed to provide the legislature with an independent source of fiscal-policy recommendations and to expedite the lengthy legislative-hearings process, received their initial trials during the 1976 session.

Numerous other reforms have been suggested as means of expediting the legislative budget process. Most take the form of placing deadlines on specific phases of legislative action. One proposal, not adopted, would have required that the general fund and education budgets be reported out of committee within five days after being submitted by the governor. Another suggestion, also not enacted, would have required passage of budget bills by the fifteenth legislative day of a regular 30-day session. In 1975, a proposed constitutional amendment would have barred legislators from receiving compensation for special sessions called to complete passage of appropriation bills. It, too, failed to receive legislative endorsement.

To cope with the problem of financial consequences of general legislation, the state Senate adopted as part of its rules the requirement that "fiscal notes" be attached to all bills requiring appropriations or affecting revenue collections.[4] Prepared by the standing committee to which the bill has been referred, the fiscal note would contain a "reliable estimate" of the amount of money involved if the legislation should be passed. The rule specifies that no bill or resolution may be given its third reading prior to passage without such a fiscal note being attached. In that event, the proposed legislation is recommitted to the Committee on Finance and Taxation. The House of Representatives has not enacted a similar requirement.

In a series of amendments to the 1976 appropriations bill, the Legislature imposed several conditions upon spending units of state government.[5] Labeled as "accountability" amendments, they inserted legislative controls and expressed legislative intent to an unprecedented degree, provoking charges of usurpation of the governor's control over state spending. The key elements halted the hiring of new state employees and the purchase of new automobiles, except for law enforcement, and allowed the legislature, rather than the governor, to allocate federal revenue-sharing funds. In addition, all departments, agencies, and institutions were required to report quarterly to the legislature, through the governor, on fund allocations and expenditures. The full impact of these assertions of legislative authority may not be known for several years. The action did, however, represent a marked departure from traditional legislative deference to the executive in Alabama's budgetary process.

Budget Staffing

At both the executive and legislative levels, staff limitations have precluded the development of extensive analytical and managerial approaches to the budget process. The attempt by the Alabama legislature to provide itself with more adequate staff capabilities was noted in the preceding pages. In this section attention will be focused on the central budget office, the Budget Division within the Department of Finance.[6]

Basically, central budget offices emphasize one of two possible orientations: control or program analysis. Because of the long-established concern with efficiency in state governments, the "watchdog" or control concept has dominated. Only in recent years—and in only a relatively few states—has the emphasis shifted to a greater concern with program analysis and management improvement. It is the "watchdog" role that has been predominant in Alabama. Usually associated with the use of the object-of-expenditure budget, this approach is primarily concerned with the close monitoring of expenditures. In such a setting, budget staffs are likely to consist almost exclusively of persons trained in accounting. The focus is on the preparation, presentation, and execution of the operating budget. Less attention is devoted to the in-depth analysis of agency management problems, program purposes, or policy development.

The functions of the central budget office in Alabama are set forth in the statute creating the Budget Division:

> To prepare and administer the budget, and direct the execution thereof. To prepare a detailed tentative budget for every department, board, bureau, commission, agency, office, and institution of the State, including those which employ special or earmarked funds . . . To make all budget allotments. To administer, enforce, and supervise the execution of the budget, including the enforcement of penalties for the violation of any law, rule, or regulation with respect thereto . . . To furnish all information for and assist in the preparation of the general revenue bill and all appropriation

bills. To prepare or make such comparison, studies and reports as may be helpful in the preparation or execution of the budget allotments or as may be required from time to time by the Director of Finance or the Governor.[7]

A tall order. To carry it out, the Budget Division had a total professional staff, at the end of 1975, of three—the budget officer and two examiners. Although increased to six professionals by early 1977, this contrasts with a staff of eighteen in Kentucky, a state of approximately the same size and level of expenditures. The small staff size alone, regardless of the training and experience of its members, precludes an extensive role in policy and program analysis. Of necessity, therefore, the Alabama budget office is restricted to a more traditional and limited function. A preliminary report of a management-consultant firm, delivered to the Governor's Committee on Fiscal Responsibility in 1975, confirmed this weakness. It noted that limited staffing in the state budget office "does not permit extensive management analysis of department expenditures or of factors affecting expenditure levels."[8] It suggested that the budget office would require at least six additional analysts (examiners) if the state were to replace its traditional budget system with a program budget.

Incrementalism

Limits of time and staff and the heavy hand of precedent have combined to produce budgetary decisions that do not vary greatly from one year to the next. As one authority on the subject has observed, "the largest determining factor of the size and content of this year's budget is last year's budget."[9] It is probably safe to say that at no stage of the budgetary process does anyone examine the full range of proposed programs and the resources available to fund them and then rationally establish a priority-ranking for all of state government. Incrementalist decision makers throughout government, in the agencies, institutions, budget office, and the legislature, tend to accept as "given" all established programs and levels of expenditure previously approved. Only those increments of change that appear unusually large are given close scrutiny. Any "new" money is distributed among a rather narrow range of competing new programs, frequently on the basis of external stimuli such as a new federal grant program or court-ordered increases in appropriations for a specific function. In Alabama in the 1970s such actions by the federal judiciary prompted increased allocations for mental-health care and prison reform. Generally, however, incremental budgeting seeks to maintain next year's appropriation for any given program at a level close to this year's expenditures.

Two factors have contributed to an incrementalist approach to budgeting in Alabama. First, the practice of convening the legislature in regular session on a biennial basis meant that agency appropriations tended to be "flat" for the second year of the biennium. Any increases were likely to appear in the first year's allocation with much smaller changes, if any, in the second year's budgets. Secondly, the heavy incidence of earmarked revenues, discussed earlier, has meant that the distribution pattern of state monies has been relatively inflexible. As additional tax collections flowed to the treasury, their use was already determined. Little opportunity existed to shift large sums from one program area to another.

There is little doubt that incrementalism has existed in state budgeting in the past. Whether it has prevailed during the inflationary period of the 1970s is the subject of considerable debate. An attempt to answer the question as it pertains to the Alabama budget was indicative, but not conclusive. The General Fund budgets of ten state agencies were examined for the period 1970–1975.[10] During this six-year period, the ten agencies averaged increases of 6.3 percent annually, only slightly greater than increases in the rate of inflation. There was, however, some considerable variation within the group, with average annual increases ranging from 4.1 to 12 percent. In addition, year-to-year increases awarded to individual agencies ranged from zero to nearly 50 percent. It should be noted, of course, that most of the agencies examined received funds from sources other than the General Fund, especially federal aid. The analysis did not include these amounts (which in a few instances were greater than state appropriations) since the purpose was to discover the extent of incrementalism in the allocation of state funds. It did appear, however, that the availability of additional federal funding often contributed to an above-average increase in state appropriations for a given agency.

Zero-base Budgeting

Dissatisfaction with existing budget procedures, especially those that contributed to incrementalism, led to several studies of the system in the mid-1970s. A legislative interim committee on finance and taxation, chaired by the lieutenant governor, examined state-agency budgets in unprecedented detail in 1975 and 1976. At the same time, the Governor's Committee on Fiscal Responsibility chartered a private accounting firm to design a wholly new budget system for the state. The State Finance Department proposed a new approach to agency budget submissions known as "zero-base budgeting." This concept was adopted in the Alabama Budget Management Act of 1976.[11]

First applied in private industry, zero-base budgeting was instituted on a limited basis by the state of Georgia in the early 1970s. It also has been implemented by several municipalities, including Washington, D.C. This approach differs from traditional budgeting in that it subjects all program funding to the same type of scrutiny as is usually applied only to new programs. As State Finance Director James R. Solomon explained it, "every department starts at zero and must identify and justify each of its programs from scratch." Under the old system, departments were required to justify only budget increases, especially those resulting from the initiation of new programs. In addition, the new law provides that departmental budget requests be broken down by activity and that each program or activity be assigned a priority ranking, thus curtailing the tendency toward "across-the-board" increases or decreases.

The purpose of the new budget approach, in the language of the act creating it, is to "further the capacity of the Governor and the Legislature to plan and finance the services which they determine the State will provide for its citizens." The system includes procedures for:

(a) the orderly establishment, continuing review, and periodic revision of the program and financial goals and policies of the State;

(b) the development, coordination, and review of long range program and financial plans that will implement established State goals and policies;

(c) the preparation, coordination, analysis and enactment of a budget, organized to focus on State services and their costs, that authorizes the implementation of policies and plans in the succeeding budget period;

(d) the evaluation of alternatives to existing policies, plans and procedures that offer potential for more efficient or effective State services; and

(e) the regular appraisal and reporting of program performance.[12]

The legislation makes clear that budget preparation and

administration is a responsibility of the governor. It also retains the requirement of a balanced budget, asserting that proposed expenditures may not exceed estimated revenues. The governor, consistent with the concept of an executive budget, is also given the responsibility for evaluating agency plans and submitting to the legislature a comprehensive financial plan for the state. Individual agencies are required to specify the goals and objectives of their respective programs and to set forth the means by which those objectives are to be met. Where agency programs are related to those of other departments of government, this relationship is to be detailed. These provisions are unique in Alabama's budgetary history.

Advocates of zero-base budgeting contend that it will enable the state's policy makers to reallocate resources from low- to high-priority programs. Basically, a management tool for evaluating departmental operations, ongoing and new, it attempts to introduce a more rational approach into the allocations process. Ideally, it would permit budget reductions in those program areas where needs had diminished or where inefficiencies were discovered, allowing the released funds to be transferred to more critical public purposes.

The Sunset Law

In the closing days of the 1976 session of the legislature, a so-called "sunset bill" received the approval of both houses and was signed by the governor.[13] This legislation, closely allied to the concept of zero-base budgeting, provides for review by a special legislative committee of each state agency, department, board, and commission every four years to determine whether it should be continued. The bill sets a possible termination date on every state agency. If a majority of both houses of the legislature and the governor concur in a committee recommendation calling for abolishing an agency, the unit would be allowed a six-month phase-out period, following which it would become extinct. Under the bill, the eleven-member committee will examine designated agencies annually, on a rotating basis, and report its recommendations to the legislature at the outset of each regular session. A legislative decision to continue or discontinue an agency will have to be made by the tenth work day of the session. A majority vote of each house plus the approval of the governor is required to terminate an agency's existence.

Whether either zero-base budgeting or sunset legislation will provide the answer to incrementalism and inflexibility in the appropriations process remains to be seen. Neither was to receive an initial test until 1977, and both on a limited basis at that time. Skeptics argue that traditional political considerations will overwhelm both efforts. With regard to zero-base budgeting, they point to the Georgia experience where, after five years, not a single program had been eliminated as a result of such review. Ongoing programs develop constituencies that resist all attempts to tamper with existing funding levels. In Georgia, the concept has been praised as an improvement over traditional budgeting, but its impact has been hampered by legislative indifference.[14]

As for Alabama's "sunset law," it may prove vulnerable to the legislative filibuster, the gubernatorial veto power, or both. In addition, once fully operational, the special review committee will be confronted with the necessity of examining annually the performance of thirty or more agencies, and it seems likely that only a few will receive full scrutiny. The magnitude of the problem became apparent in late 1976 as the eleven-member legislative committee prepared for the first round of agency reviews. The law required that all agencies not specifically mentioned in the bill be examined by October, 1978. According to the committee's chairman, some 300 units of government fell into this category, including institutions of higher education. It appeared doubtful that the committee and the small legislative fiscal office staff could adequately review the performance of so many organizations in the two-year time span provided by the legislation. The 1977 session of the legislature faced more than 200 resolutions dealing with agency renewals, including recommendations that nineteen small units be abolished.[15]

Gubernatorial Control

From its inception, the state budget movement has been tied to efforts to improve the executive management of public affairs. Combined with such other turn-of-the-century reforms as the "short ballot" and "integration" of the administrative system under control of the chief executive, budgeting was viewed as a means for improving the efficiency of state government.[16] If the governor was to be the chief executive, in fact as well as title, he must be given the tools of management, and this would mean control over the state's fiscal affairs. The quest for executive leadership was a reaction against the nineteenth-century philosophy of popular government and limitations on governmental authority. It was, in addition, a response to the inefficiencies and occasional corruptions associated at that time with legislative dominance of state government.

The new powers vested in the governor by the Alabama constitution of 1901 to estimate revenues and submit the details of a general revenue bill was a step in the direction of gubernatorial leadership. Subsequent changes leading to the establishment of a Department of Finance and a Budget Division under the governor's control enhanced his position. But it would be misleading to conclude that these changes, in themselves, led to executive domination of the budget process. In Alabama, as elsewhere, numerous restrictions remained on the discretionary authority of the chief executive to impose his will on budgetary matters. As applied to nearly all the states, these limitations have been summarized by Frederick C. Mosher:

> The constraints upon governors in virtually all of the states which are imposed by traditions, constitutions, laws, professional-bureaucratic interests, private interests and federal grants leave minimal room for maneuver. The great bulk of states' budgets is mandatory, a fact which most new incoming governors learn quickly to their dismay. In most states, large shares of expenditures are not covered in the budget at all, and in a few the budget comprehends less than one quarter of the state's finances.[17]

These comments are particularly applicable to Alabama. The state's heavy reliance upon federal grants, the extensive earmarking of revenues for exclusive uses, and the exclusion from the General Fund budget of some 90 percent of all expenditures, contribute to a minimization of gubernatorial control. In addition, the state possesses one of the most fragmented administrative structures to be found anywhere. More than 200 distinct administrative units—departments, agencies, boards, and commissions—can be identified, many of them operating largely with funds that are not included in the executive budget.[18] Given this complex arrangement, Alabama's governors have found it necessary to seek control over administration—including budgetary control—through informal, "political" processes rather than by the use of more formal devices.

As in the more distant past, recent proposals for "reforming" the state budget process have centered on strengthening the role of the governor. In some states, budget reform has been linked to efforts to develop a comprehensive statewide planning function in the governor's office. In a few states, these efforts have been combined with extensive reorganizations of the executive branch. The next chapter will examine developments in this direction in Alabama.

6

Toward a Program Budget

The way in which financial information is presented determines to a great extent the kinds of budgetary decisions that are made. The inclusion or exclusion of various types of revenue and expenditure data, even the context in which such information is displayed, is based largely upon the purpose that the budget is designed to serve. It has been suggested that all budgets reflect an emphasis on one of three possible functions: control, management, or planning.[1]

While all budget documents encompass some combination of these purposes, most can be found to be primarily concerned with one over the others. If the emphasis is on controlling expenditures, the budget form most likely to be employed is the so-called object-of-expenditure or line-item budget. Where a management orientation is present, as in many municipal governments, a "performance" budget frequently will be found. If the budget is seen as a part of a broader planning process, linked closely to top-level policy making, a "program" budget may be utilized. This type takes numerous forms and frequently contains many of the elements associated with the first two types. During the past decade, many state governments have moved in the direction of program budgeting. Alabama has been no exception.

The Line-Item Budget

From its inception, Alabama's executive budget has been

presented in object-of-expenditure form. The original budget act called for presenting appropriation requests in detail for each general class of funds and by organization units, indicating the amounts to be spent for operation, maintenance, administration, and capital projects. As amended in 1939, the law required that agency requests be broken down into (a) salaries, (b) travel, (c) administration, operation, and maintenance expenses, and (d) the purchase of land, public improvements, and other capital outlays.[2] More recent adaptations set forth in detail, under the general heading "other expenses," such items as: supplies and materials; postage, telephone and telegraph; travel expense; printing and binding; motor vehicle operations; heat, light, water and power; repairs and alterations; insurance and bonding; rental of equipment and premises, and assorted other expenditures peculiar to an agency's operations. Salaries are listed by position. Equipment purchases and capital outlays are itemized under separate headings. Figure 8 illustrates a typical budget presentation under this form.

The line-item or "object" classification was a direct product of an era in which legislators and the general public distrusted administrators.[3] By establishing detailed listings of things for which public funds were being expended and by linking each category of spending to a specific account, tight control could be exerted over the bureaucracy. That was the principal purpose of the system: to control expenditures at the agency and departmental levels. As one student of budgeting has noted:

> Where the objects of outlay are specified in detail, and where the budget as adopted by the legislature incorporates this detail, the administrative discretion of department heads is greatly reduced. The object detail, by its very nature, limits the freedom of administrative action.[4]

By detailing the objects of expenditure, this type of budget

FIGURE 8

Object-of-Expenditure Budget*

Actual 1972-73	Estimated 1973-74	OBJECT	1974–75 Agency Request	1974–75 Governor's Recommendation
x x x	x x x	**SALARIES**	x x x	x x x
		Director		
		Asst. Director		
		Exec. Assistant		
		Accountant I		
		Accountant II		
		Clerk-Steno I		
		Planner I		
		Information Spec.		
		Etc.		
		TOTAL SALARIES		
		OTHER EXPENSES		
		Supplies & Materials		
		Postage, Telephone		
		Travel Expense		
		Motor Vehicle Operations		
		Utilities		
		Rentals		
		Rentals		
		Janitorial Services		
		Equipment Maintenance		
		Miscellaneous		
		TOTAL OTHER EXPENSES		
		EQUIPMENT PURCHASES		
		Office Equipment		
		Motor Vehicle Equipment		
		TOTAL EQUIPMENT		
x x x	x x x	**GRAND TOTALS**	x x x	x x x

*Illustrative only. Actual Figures Omitted.

and accounting system stresses means rather than ends, the resource inputs and organizational structures rather than the purposes or achievements of government.[5] As a means of assuring accountability and encouraging efficiency, such budgets work quite well. By setting forth salaries and other costs associated with each position in the government, the line-item budget enables reviewing authorities, including legislators, to keep a hand in personnel decisions. It also permits comparisons to be made across agency lines, since most units of government share many common items of expenditure. In addition, the itemization of spending facilitates auditing that is primarily concerned with the legality of expenditures.

The persistence of object-of-expenditure budgeting in state governments throughout the country reflects, to a considerable extent, the belief that close control saves money. It may also reveal the continuation of the view widely held in the early reform era that the principal purpose of a budget system is to control abuses in the expenditure of public funds.[6] This type of budget is usually found, as in Alabama, linked to other control devices. These include central-budget-office allotment controls, authority to require the setting aside of reserves in agency appropriations, requirements that internal agency fund transfers be approved by the central budget office (in Alabama, the director of finance), and budget-office approval of purchase orders.

As the emphasis in state government has shifted from the exercising of controls to obtaining and measuring program results, the object-type budget has been found wanting. While most state budget officials still view control as their most important responsibility, the public and elected officials have become increasingly concerned about what was being accomplished with those line-item inputs.[7] The basic weakness of the line-item budget is that it cannot, as presently constructed, provide answers to questions having to do with managerial effectiveness or program results. To know that Agency "A" spent $12,000 on staff travel last year and would like to spend $15,000 for the same purpose next year does not provide much insight as to whether such expenditures have contributed anything to achieving the agency's objectives. Indeed, the traditional line-item or object-of-expenditure budget does not require a statement as to what the agency's objectives may be. In the absence of such information, little means exist by which to measure the extent to which any given expenditure relates to program performance. For this reason, object-type budgeting has been said to contribute to the general practice of incrementalism in state government. Past appropriations provide the "base" from which future budget requests are projected.

Dissatisfaction with the limited informational capacities of the traditional budget led in the 1960s to a movement for change in the way financial data were presented. Efforts to incorporate measures of work performance had led to experimentation with the so-called "performance" budget earlier. Although enjoying some success in municipal governments, where activities such as police work and refuse collection lent themselves to quantification, the performance budget movement did not gain wide acceptance among state governments.[8] Only during the past decade, encouraged by similar efforts at the national level, have state governments seriously undertaken budgetary change. This has taken the form of various adaptations of what was initially referred to as the "Planning-Programming-Budgeting System," or PPBS, for short. Before examining the move toward program budgeting in Alabama, a brief look at PPBS might help trace the evolution of this new concept.

Planning–Programming–Budgeting Systems (PPBS)

Although the idea of an executive budget had originated at the state and local levels of government early in this century, subsequent departures from the traditional routines of budgeting usually have had their beginnings at the national level. Such was the case with the most recent innovation in public financial management—the creation of a planning-programming-budgeting system in the early 1960s. Conceived by the RAND Corporation and first adopted by the United States Air Force, this novel approach gained acceptance throughout the Department of Defense during Robert McNamara's tenure as secretary of defense. From there, it spread via executive order and Bureau of the Budget mandate throughout the executive branch of the federal government.[9] Based on a rational model of the decision-making process, PPBS was an attempt to link the administrative functions of planning and budgeting. Previously, these two functions had taken place in most organizations—including the Department of Defense—as separate, distinct, and seldom coordinated activities.

PPBS is rooted intellectually in the discipline of economics. Concerned with the allocation of limited resources, including money, economists subscribe to a few basic principles—that there are always alternative ways of achieving agreed-upon goals and that the comparison of alternatives, especially at the margin, is essential to choosing the "right" way to do a job or use resources; that most situations pose the problem of "trade-offs" or substitution possibilities; and that in order to make the "best" choice it is necessary to compare the costs and the benefits associated with each possible alternative. Although numerous variations exist, the "rational model" of decision making usually includes the following steps:

1) Identify the problem and understand it;
2) Define and clarify the goals being sought;
3) Pose alternatives for the attainment of the goals;
4) Analyze the anticipated consequences of each major alternative; and

5) Appraise the alternatives and choose.[10]

In the area of financial decisions, advocates of PPBS insisted upon comprehensiveness and the systematic appraisal of all costs and benefits. By comprehensiveness was meant that *all* relevant values and alternatives associated with each public goal be entered into the calculation. In weighing the costs and benefits of alternative policies or programs, an efficiency criterion was injected into the equation. Choice was to be based largely on an estimate of how each alternative would contribute to achieving the objective at the least cost. Social, psychological, and political costs and benefits, although difficult to quantify, were also to be taken into consideration in arriving at decisions.

The new system has been defined as one that requires: (1) the precise identification of program objectives, (2) the establishment of criteria to be used to measure the accomplishment of objectives, (3) the formalized consideration of alternative methods of accomplishing program objectives, and (4) the estimation of the costs and accomplishments predicted under each alternative method.[11] If, for example, within the broad governmental goal of "developing human resources," one objective is to reduce the rate of adult illiteracy, a remedial reading program might be established. The objective is fairly clear. Designing criteria to measure accomplishment would not appear difficult; e.g., the use of tests to determine reading and writing skills before and after completion of the instruction. It is possible, however, that several methods could be employed to achieve the objective, thus suggesting alternative programs (home tutorials, for example, as opposed to group instruction). Cost estimates could be compiled along with projections of success rates, utilization of the service, availability of instructional personnel, convenience to clients, and other factors that might enter into the decision. With such information at hand, a choice could be made. All costs associated with the selected program would then be incorporated into the administering unit's budget figures. Periodic assessments of program output or accomplishment would provide the basis for future decisions, including the possibilities of additional or substitute approaches to the problem. Although greatly oversimplified, these are the basic steps in the PPBS process.

Rather than as a shopping list of things to be bought by agencies of government, PPBS designers saw the budget more as an information-and-decision process. Once in place, it would enable top-level policy-makers to make more rational choices. In this system, spending decisions would be based on "output" categories rather than "inputs." Not how much money an agency wanted for salaries, travel, or equipment, but the total cost of goods and services actually delivered to citizens would become the basis for decision.[12] Spending would be linked to the goals, objectives, and end products of government. The purposes of government would become more important than the processes. Specific programs would be related to broad public policy goals. Those programs, and their associated costs, that contributed best to attainment of these goals would be preferred. In addition, PPBS proposed for the first time to place budgetary decisions within a time frame extending beyond the next fiscal year (or two years, in the case of some state governments). It would do this by extending the time horizon at least five years into the future. In theory, at least, this would require agencies to think in terms of total program costs over time. Under traditional budgeting, future costs of present decisions are often ignored, perhaps deliberately. With longer-term projections of costs, both chief executives and legislators would be in a position to make more informed choices among competing programs.

The new planning-programming-budgeting system, then, possessed the characteristics of being future-oriented, comprehensive, and tied to means-ends analysis. This was in contrast to traditional forms of budgeting, which tend to be repetitive, input-oriented, incremental, and short-term. The cornerstone of the new system was its requirement that agencies and departments of government identify their objectives and systematically analyze alternative ways to achieve them. Essential to the process was a commitment to a form of systems analysis that was variously labelled as "cost-benefit analysis," "cost-utility analysis," and "cost-effectiveness analysis." Although not ruling out the use of qualitative information, the emphasis clearly was on quantitative data.

Instituted on a governmentwide basis in the mid-1960s, PPBS expired on June 21, 1971, a passing scarcely mourned throughout the federal bureaucracy. The noble experiment, while stirring much intellectual ferment for a decade, had failed. The reasons were many.[13] The information and analytical capabilities required to make the system work simply did not exist in many segments of the government. Congress, never brought fully into the partnership in the experiment, did not accept it, continuing to appropriate on the basis of traditional budgetary presentations. By insisting on cross-program comparisons, PPBS cast a spotlight on inconsistencies and duplications. By placing programs and agencies in a position of competing with each other for funding, it escalated budgetary conflicts. Meaningful analysis was limited by problems in defining the real objectives of many programs, as well as by the existence of multiple and noncomparable benefits. Additional difficulties arose in considering a time stream of costs and benefits, as opposed to the evaluation of costs and benefits for a single point in time, as in traditional budgeting. For these reasons, and many more, the Office of Management and Budget discontinued the system as part of "continuing efforts to simplify budget submission requirements."[14]

PPBS: The State Experience

The introduction of programming-planning-budgeting systems was not confined to the national government. State governments and even a few local governments were caught up in the experiment. State agencies that drew heavily upon federal grants to finance their activities often were required to submit budgetary data in PPBS form to federal administering agencies. In Alabama, for example, the Department of Conservation and Natural Resources and the Health Department were drawn into PPBS in this manner. Other states, for reasons of their own, attempted to apply the new system.

In 1967, a cooperative effort between the Bureau of the Budget, George Washington University, and the Ford Foundation led to the enlistment of five states, five counties, and five cities in the so-called "5–5–5 project."[15] The purpose of this demonstration project was to determine the feasibility of instituting PPBS in state and local governments. The five participating states were California, Michigan, New York, Vermont, and Wisconsin. Although not included in the project, the states of Hawaii and Pennsylvania undertook similar efforts while Arkansas, at the initiative of its governor, relied on consultants from the RAND Corporation to study the feasibility of introducing PPBS into that state's legislatively dominated budget process.[16] As might be expected, the results were mixed. Certain lessons were learned, however, especially from the closely monitored 5–5–5 experiences.

One assessment of the impact of PPBS in states which had introduced it concluded that "innovation has been very limited and . . . the mode of budget choice has not been significantly changed."[17] By the early 1970s the movement toward program budgeting of this type had slowed noticeably. Program structures remained unused, analytical studies had not been incorporated into decision processes, and legislatures had not embraced the new concept. Prevailing budgetary traditions seemed to have overcome efforts at innovation.

There were, of course, exceptions. It has been generally acknowledged that a few states—California, Hawaii, and Wisconsin among them—succeeded in establishing versions of PPBS as integral parts of the budget process. Even in those states where full implementation was never achieved or where, as in New York, it was formally abandoned, residual effects remain. The practice of looking at multiyear projections of costs, for example, and the effort to consider the activities of state government in broad, program terms rather than in narrow, agency-defined categories can be traced back to the PPBS experiment. What can be concluded is that in most states where the new system was tried it produced changes in the traditional budget process. The nature of those changes varied from one state to another.

Those who have analyzed the attempt to introduce PPBS at the state level draw certain general conclusions:

1) The support of the chief executive is essential. Without it, adequate resources will not be channeled into the new system.

2) The full support of professional career employees throughout the government is necessary. A doubting bureaucracy can be fatal to any major innovation such as PPBS.

3) Where the new PPBS analysts were separated from the existing budget staff and operation, analysis had minimal input into budgetary decision making.

4) The program format may be viewed by legislators as a threat to their control over the pursestrings and as an obstruction to the legislative oversight function. Where budget reform has succeeded, as in California and Hawaii, legislative support has been a critical factor.

5) Excessive fragmentation of the existing state adminis-

trative structure hinders budget innovation. PPBS, with its centralizing tendencies, posed a threat to agency autonomy.

6) Where the bulk of a state's budget is mandated by previous decisions (earmarking) and many expenditures are not covered by the budget, the impact of PPBS on spending decisions will be diluted.

The lessons of experience, thus, suggest that certain conditions are desirable as prerequisites for installing a program budgeting system. Briefly summarized, these include: support by the governor, the legislature, and the career professionals in the bureaucracy; a merging of planners, program analysts and budgeters at the highest staff levels; administrative reorganization when the functions of government are dispersed throughout a fragmented and uncoordinated bureaucracy; and the inclusion in the budget of all expenditures, suggesting the "unearmarking" of funds where possible. This is not to imply that program budgeting cannot be implemented unless all these conditions are present. Experience has shown, however, that the chances of success are increased if all or most of them exist or can be brought about in connection with the adoption of program budgeting.

Alabama Developments

In 1974, the Governor's Committee on Fiscal Responsibility contracted with the private accounting firm of Ernst and Ernst to design a new budget system for Alabama. The need for improved financial management practices had been implicit in a twelve-week study of state agencies and institutions in 1972. That study, known as the governor's cost-control survey, had pinpointed deficiencies in administrative organization and procedures which, it was estimated, were costing the state more than $100 million a year. In the wake of that report, the Committee on Fiscal Responsibility was formed to develop new budget methods designed to provide a better accounting of how the state was spending its money.

Although the final report of the consulting firm was not available at this writing, press reports of early drafts and statements of those close to the study provided considerable information about what was being contemplated. Indeed, many of the basic concepts of the proposed program budget were incorporated in the budgeting bill enacted by the legislature in 1976. Basically, the recommendation was that a program budgeting system be introduced gradually to replace the traditional line-item budget in use in Alabama for the past forty-five years. The change was to be made incrementally, with the state Health Department designated as the "lead" agency, beginning the process of transforming its budget presentation into a program format with the 1976/77 fiscal year. Other departments were to follow suit in subsequent years. Adoption of zero-base budgeting in 1976, however, had the effect of speeding up the transition by requiring program-type information from all agencies, starting with the 1978 fiscal year. Initially, both types of budgets, line-item and program, were to be prepared. Indeed, program budgeting in those states which have adopted it has not led to abandonment of object-of-expenditure data. The effect, however, is to relegate such information to a secondary position with budgetary decisions being based primarily upon program data.

The initial report of the consulting firm also recommended that agency budgets be made inclusive. That is, budget documents should include all agency funds, from whatever source they may be derived, including federal grant monies. As noted earlier, one of the weaknesses of the Alabama budget has been the absence of most federal funds from the presentation. This had the effect of excluding from the legislative review process more than one-quarter of all state revenues.

More importantly, the proposed program budget would inject into the financial decision process the requirement that government agencies identify their programs by purpose, define specific objectives, and relate the costs of their operation to the attainment of those goals. As the manager of the consulting firm put it: "We need to look at the activities of each agency, the service it performs, and tie that to its costs."[18] Further, such costs under the new system would be projected over a three-to-five year period, not just estimated for the next fiscal year, or biennium, as under the old system.

The key to program budgeting within state government is the identification of basic program "packages." The government of Alabama consists of more than 150 distinct administrative units—more than 300, if institutions are treated separately. It is virtually impossible, however, to grasp the scope, purpose, and product of state government if it is viewed solely within the framework of the organization chart. There simply are not 150 separate and mutually exclusive functions of government. Rather, there are approximately that many agencies conducting a considerably larger number of programs, most of which can be grouped for purposes of analysis into ten or fewer categories. These categories, such as "education" or "public health" or "transportation," spill across agency jurisdictional boundaries. Thus, one survey of Alabama's administrative organization revealed thirty-five different agencies, boards, commissions, and institutions involved in providing public health services or contributing in some way to that function.[19]

Most program-oriented studies of state government suggest the existence of from seven to ten broad program categories. Alabama's program structure has been divided into eight broad functional areas, grouping related programs. Goal statements have been attached to each of the eight program areas, as follows:

I. *Economic Development and Regulation.*

Goal: To encourage economic development in Alabama at greater than the national average, but at the same time protect and conserve natural and human resources to the best extent possible.

II. *Education and Cultural Resources.*

Goal: To assure that every citizen has the opportunity to obtain a basic education and to afford every citizen the opportunity to pursue further educational and cultural improvement according to his individual needs.

III. *Natural Resources and Recreation.*

Goal: To develop a natural resources program which will enhance and protect the natural environment for the social and economic betterment of the entire state. Provide a comprehensive recreational program that provides indoor and outdoor recreational and leisure time opportunities.

IV. *Health—Physical and Mental.*

Goal: To provide the means and opportunity for all citizens to meet their health needs through the expansion and the improvement of the quality and quantity of health services.

V. *Social Services.*

Goal: To improve and extend social services to all citizens through increased government participation.

VI. *Protection of Persons and Property.*

Goal: To assure that all citizens are secure from the threat of crime and provide maximum protection from unfair trade practices and natural disaster.

VII. *Transportation.*

Goal: To promote the development of an improved, balanced transportation system (air, water, land) which emphasizes the use of existing facilities.

VIII. *General Government.*

Goal: To improve the delivery of services and utilize resources in the most effective manner possible.[20]

These program definitions and goal statements provided the framework for Alabama's initial step into the world of program budgeting in late 1976. This effort will be examined in more detail below. First, however, a brief look at some of the principal implications and problems associated with any attempt to impose a program budgeting system on an existing administrative and financial management structure.

Administrative Reorganization

Efforts to implement program budgeting are burdened by numerous conceptual, as well as practical and political, problems. In situations, like that prevailing in Alabama, where state government expanded on an ad hoc basis over a long period of time, there is little coherence in the organizational structure. Related activities, nominally falling within the same program category, are dispersed among many administratively unrelated units of government. Placement of these activities within general program areas is difficult and may be accomplished, at times, only through arbitrary assignment. Are medical schools properly placed within the "health" category, or that of "education?" Is the dental-hygiene program of the public-school system an educational or public-health function? How are the objectives of such activities determined? By whom? To which program area are the costs to be assigned? If dental hygiene is essentially a public-health activity, should administrative and financial control over it be placed in the Department of Health? Can program budgeting take place in the absence of extensive administrative reorganization? The answer seems to be yes. The proposed budget system for Alabama does not urge reorganization. Programs will be treated within organizational contexts that already exist, at least for the present.[21]

Administrative reorganization was viewed as a panacea for the ills of state government long before program budgeting became popular. The idea is at least as old as Governor Frank Lowden's reform of Illinois government in 1917. Since 1965, reorganizations of varying degrees have taken place in about fifteen states. Some, as in Louisiana, Florida, and North Carolina, have come about as the result of constitutional revision. Most of the others have been the result of legislative action. A few reorganizations, as in Kentucky and California, were brought about by executive order subject to legislative approval. In all cases, the reforms have centered around a reduction in the number of departments and an integration of the administrative units of government to provide for more direct control by the governor. In Massachusetts, for example, a new program-management system brought 176 agencies together under just nine cabinet-level departments, each department head reporting directly to the governor.[22]

Program budgeting consists of grouping together all expenditures having the same purpose, regardless of which agencies spend the money or what types of goods are purchased. While the states that have adopted program budgeting have generally used it to supplement conventional budgets, any move toward program budgeting spotlights the need for administrative reorganization. Those who have examined Alabama's financial administration practices in recent years have reached agreement on the need for reorganization. The coordinator of the 1972 cost-control survey, for example, suggested a vast reorganization of the 140 principal state agencies into just five departments reporting directly to the governor.[23] A Chicago-based management firm, in a preliminary report to the governor's Committee on State Government Reorganization, labeled Alabama's government "a fragmented system composed of more than 210 agency heads'' and recommended that all existing agencies become subdivisions of not more than twenty key departments reporting directly to the governor.[24] Lieutenant-Governor Jere Beasley, chairman of a legislative budget-control subcommittee, said his group had identified more than 400 units of state government and suggested that the number could be reduced to between twenty-five and thirty-five major state agencies.[25]

During the 1977 session of the legislature, two bills were introduced aimed at drastically revising the administrative organization of state government. One proposed bill, backed by the governor, would have reduced the number of executive departments to fifteen, each headed by a secretary appointed by the governor. The other, sponsored by Senator Bill King of Huntsville, would have provided for only six ''super-agencies'' directly responsible to the governor. More than 100 agencies would have been abolished or merged under both proposals. Both bills bogged down in disputes over the mechanics of implementation, however, and the legislature adjourned without enacting either proposal.

Earmarking

As noted previously, a disproportionate amount of Alabama's state budget is earmarked by law for specific purposes. Some 90 percent of the state's revenues are thus set aside for particular uses and cannot be transferred easily to other functions of government. The effect is to create a system of ''mandatory'' appropriations for a wide range of programs and a large number of governmental agencies. Advocates of program budgeting invariably favor the ''un-earmarking'' of revenues. However, this is not easily accomplished since it requires legislative action and, in some cases, constitutional amendments to bring it about. Agencies funded by earmarked revenues and interest groups benefiting from the services of such agencies can be expected to resist efforts to place earmarked monies into a general fund. Federal categorical grant funds also constitute "earmarked" money, but control over the disposition of grant funds is outside the province of state government. One of the recommendations of the consulting firm designing a new budget system for Alabama was to include all funds in the budget documents, something not done previously. However, placing such expenditures in the budget is not the same as giving control over them to the governor or the legislature. There is general agreement that the adoption of a program budget implies the need to "unearmark" revenues. Failure to do so would leave intact most of the existing budgetary allocations and would reduce program budgeting to a mere manipulation of techniques—form for form's sake.[26]

The Link to State Planning

Advocates of program budgeting view it as a means of bringing together two traditionally separated governmental functions, budgeting and planning. Budgeting, in its program version, contributes importantly to the policy-coordinative aspect of state planning, better enabling the chief executive to manage the delivery of services by state government. Much has been written over the past thirty years about the interdependence of planners and budgeters.[27] But different orientations kept the two activities apart. As one observer described it, "budgeters were preoccupied with the continuing routines of government operation; planners with the processes of change."[28] Planners committed their visions of the future to paper without due regard for the costs of what was contemplated. Budget practitioners were primarily concerned with rationing available resources within the context of ongoing programs. In short, budgeting has been conservative and constraining while planning has been innovative and expansionist.[29]

Both planning and budgeting have changed in recent years. Planners have broadened their horizons beyond traditional concerns with physical development to include an interest in statewide "comprehensive" planning as a means of bringing about policy coordination at the highest levels of state government.[30] This new orientation is designed to facilitate executive control over the far-flung and fragmented administrative structure of the state. The function of planners, in this view, is to assist the governor in managing "the complexity, overlaps, gaps, conflicts, and confusions of various unlike services."[31] Policy coordination, to be successful, must link planning to budgeting. However, the marriage can be successful only if both functions are well established within the jurisdiction of the state's chief executive. Program budgeting, with its multi-year perspective and attention to agency objectives, is clearly more future-oriented than traditional budgeting approaches.

The Alabama Development Office (ADO), the state planning agency, is strategically located as a staff agency to the governor. Its concerns, however, have fallen largely within the context of "traditional" state planning: the provision of technical assistance to local governments and efforts to promote economic development. Although it has produced a limited number of "policy-oriented" studies, ADO has not developed a policy-planning orientation. Further, it has not, as yet, established any clearly defined relationship to the budgetary process. Planning within the framework of a program budget, therefore, is most likely to occur *within* departments and agencies, not on a more comprehensive basis encompassing statewide concerns. Such an approach is consistent with the view that program budgeting, at least initially, should not violate existing agency jurisdictional boundaries. The budget, in short, should be "the key planning and financial management tool of *the agency*."[32] Expenditures can be planned on a program basis—within each agency or institution—giving consideration to agency priorities, available revenues, and alternative approaches to providing services.

The use of the program budget to join together expenditure analysis and statewide comprehensive planning at a level transcending agency boundaries would appear to lie well into the future. Its potential as a policy coordinating and decision-making tool of the governor seems doubtful in Alabama owing to the problems of administrative fragmentation, earmarking of revenues, and separation of statewide planning from the budget process.

Implementing the 1976 Budget Act

In the closing days of its 1976 regular session, the Alabama legislature enacted the most far-reaching reform of the state's budget process since 1939. The Budget Management Act of 1976 was an attempt "to establish a comprehensive system for budgeting and financial management which furthers the capacity of the Governor and the Legislature to plan and finance the services which they determine the State will provide for its citizens."[33] More than that, it represented a departure from the historical reliance upon a line-item or object-of-expenditure budget and launched state government in the direction of program budgeting. Although billed as "zero-base" budgeting, the program format was made clear in subsequent directives issued by the Division of the Budget. The act, itself, stipulated that agencies henceforth would be required to establish program and financial goals, evaluate alternatives to existing policies, and prepare budgets that would focus on services and their costs.

Governor George C. Wallace, in a memorandum to all department heads and budget officials, spelled out the new requirements:

> The severe financial conditions that have been facing state government in Alabama require that we take a new approach to the budget making process. . . . For the first time, I am

asking all department heads to state explicitly their overall program priorities for ongoing activities as well as priorities for any requested changes in funding levels.

The zero based budgeting process requires documentation of goals and objectives of the various departments of state government and includes methods to associate costs to carry out those goals and objectives. Each department will be required to determine cost by activity and to rank the activity in priority order.[34]

To implement the new approach, a five-level program structure was designed to guide agency budget preparation, as follows:

Function—The highest aggregation of related governmental services directed to achieving broad statewide goals. (Eight functional areas and their goals were identified earlier in this chapter).

Major Program Area—A grouping of related governmental services directed to achieving specific statewide goals.

Program—The specific governmental services required to achieve a specific objective. A program is directed to meeting the needs of an identified clientele (or group of recipients or beneficiaries).

Program Element—A further breakdown of the program into key budgetable parts, consisting of the group of related services required to achieve a specific program objective.

Program Element Activity—A grouping of the related tasks performed by the organizational units to provide a specific service to identified clientele or beneficiaries. It is the lowest level for practical budgetary application.[35]

To illustrate the above breakdown, an example from the Department of Public Health can be used. (See Figure 9.)

Function—"Health—Physical and Mental"
Major Program Area—"Physical Health"
Program—"Environmental Health Program"

FIGURE 9
Compilation of Department Budget Program Basis
Source Alabama Department of Finance, Division
of the Budget, "Budget Forms and Instructions"
1976.

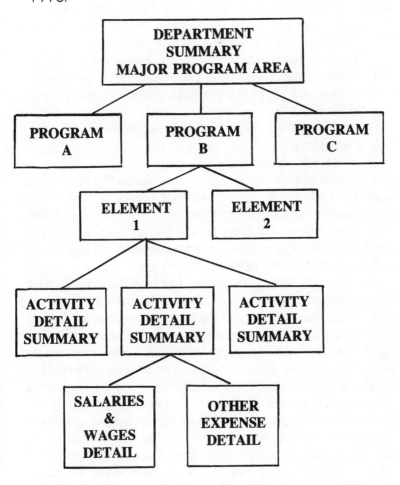

Program Element—"Inspection Services"
Activities—"Conduct food surveys," "Inspect and rate
food service establishments," "Provide sani-
tary food instructions to lunchroom employees," etc.

Agency appropriation requests are to be tied to each "activity." Cost figures within each activity category are to be
based on seven types of expenditures, as follows:[36]

1) Personnel costs (salaries, wages, etc.)
2) Services purchased (rentals, professional fees, etc.)
3) Products purchased (office supplies, repair parts, etc.)
4) Grants and benefits (retirement benefits, medical services, etc.)
5) Capital outlays (land, buildings, equipment)
6) Debt service
7) Interfund expenditures

This expenditure detail will be retained in the requesting
agencies. Only the aggregated costs for each "activity" will
be submitted with the budget request. However, this information must be available for review by the Budget Division,
the Legislative Fiscal Office, or members of the legislature
and other authorized persons.[37]

Adoption of a program budget has implications for both
accounting and reporting systems within state government.
It is the accounting system which provides the link between
that which has been planned or programmed and actual
performance.[38] Accounting provides the mechanism
through which top management can determine the extent to
which program decisions have been carried out. To meet this
requirement, a new statewide "expenditure chart of accounts" was devised to complement the budget system.[39]
The expenditure object codes include the seven listed above
plus an eighth category: "nonexpenditure disbursements."
This would include such transactions as employee withhold-
ings for income tax, Social Security taxes, health-insurance

premiums, certain tax refunds, disbursements of resources for investment purposes, and payments of monies collected and held by the state in a trust capacity, such as performance bonds. In addition to the eight major expenditure object titles, the initial version of the new expenditure chart listed eighty separate subsidiary objects, and some 380 specific object categories. Thus, the detailed breakdown of the accounting system continued to reflect the strong control emphasis in Alabama's budgeting system.

The First Year

In Alabama, as elsewhere, the zero-base concept was launched in an effort to rationalize the budget process and to reduce the incrementalist nature of traditional budgeting. Budgeting for the 1978 fiscal year was accomplished under the new procedures and a preliminary assessment of results is possible. For the first time, departments, agencies, and institutions were required to examine critically entire programs, not just incremental changes in ongoing activities. In 1977, also for the first time, requesting agencies were required to report all sources of revenue, including federal funds and special earmarked revenues. Unlike the traditional "numbers only" budgets of the past, the new approach allowed departments to submit detailed narrative justifications of programs, plans, priorities, and alternatives to be considered. Although some of those responsible for agency budget preparation complained of the vastly increased amount of paperwork, the new approach provided reviewing authorities with previously unavailable program data on which to base appropriation recommendations.

The 1977 legislative session revealed, however, that what went into effect under the label, "zero-base budget" was, in fact, a relatively simple version of a program budget. As has been the case wherever the concept was introduced, the term "zero-base" has proved to be a misnomer. No one

actually insists on starting at base zero, i.e., no appropriations at all. If such were the case, there would be no need for
a "sunset" law. Those agencies funded at zero would simply
expire for lack of life-sustaining infusions of money. There is
no evidence that any agency presented a budget request
containing a zero-level alternative.

The critical question that remains unanswered is whether
final appropriations would have varied in the absence of the
new budget format. With the bulk of state funds contained in
special, earmarked categories and the heavy dependence
upon federal grant monies, the amount available for discretionary allocation remains small. In a total budget of some
$2.5 billion for 1978, less than $200 million was appropriated
to the general fund. In addition, certain programs, such as
state aid to local governments and public schools, are financed according to statutory formulas that do not lend
themselves to the zero-base approach. A literal, across-
the-board, zero-base review of all state programs probably is
not possible within the framework of an annual budget cycle.[40] The result is that decision makers tend to concentrate
on a relatively small number of issues and programs. This
appears to have been the case during the first year of Alabama's experience with this novel approach to budgeting.

Alabama's present budget system can fairly be described,
at this writing, as being "in transition." The adoption of a
"zero-base" or program budget in 1976 represented a radical
departure from the traditional object-of-expenditure budget
that had evolved over the previous seventy-five years. How
successful the new approach will prove to be, in the face of
various structural and legal impediments, remains to be
seen. Most observers agree that a new budgeting system
requires at least five years of operation before a reasonable
evaluation can be made. What can be said at this point,
however, is that Alabama's policy makers in both the execu-

tive and legislative branches of government responded positively to the financial management crisis that faced the state in the mid-1970s. The new approach to budgeting represents an effort to come to grips with the problem of effectively managing public funds in an era of rapidly escalating costs and growing resistance to increased taxation.

Appendix

Alabama's Budget Calendar

August 1–September 1	Budget Division prepares Budget Manual, Instructions, and Forms and distributes to Departments.
September 1–December 1	Departments prepare budget requests.
November 1	Budget requests of $500,000 or less due in Budget Office and Legislative Fiscal Office.
December 1	Budget requests of more than $500,000 due in Budget Office and Legislative Fiscal Office.
November 1–January 1	Finance Department, Budget Office, and Legislative Fiscal Office review of Departmental budget requests. Revenue estimates prepared.
November 1–February 1	Governor's comprehensive program budget and financial plan prepared.
At least two weeks prior to legislative session	Departmental budget hearings
By 5th Legislative day	Governor submits budget to Legislature
February 1–May 16	Legislative review, analysis, and adoption of budget.

Immediately following adoption by Legislature	Departments prepare operational plans, subject to approval by Finance Dept.
October 1	Fiscal Year begins.

Source: Alabama Department of Finance, Budget Division, "Budget Calendar" (Montgomery: 1976) (mimeographed).

Notes

Chapter One

1. Jesse Burkhead, *Government Budgeting* (New York: John Wiley & Sons, Inc., 1956), pp. 6–7. Chapter One contains an excellent summary of the development of budgeting in Europe and the United States. A more detailed history of budgeting may be found in A. E. Buck, *The Budget in Governments of Today* (New York: The MacMillan Co., 1934), Chapter 1.

2. For a more thorough discussion of the budget as a "political" document, see Aaron Wildavsky, *The Politics of the Budgetary Process* (Boston: Little, Brown & Company, 1974).

3. See, for example, Alabama, Office of the Governor, *Governor's Cost Control Survey Study and Recommendations* (Montgomery: August, 1972).

Chapter Two

1. *Official Proceedings of the Constitutional Convention of the State of Alabama, May 21st, 1901 to September 3rd, 1901* (Wetumpka, Ala.: Wetumpka Printing Co., 1940), Vol. II, pp. 2423–501.

2. This discussion of the early years of budgeting in Alabama draws heavily upon two sources: Paul E. Alyea, *Alabama's Balancing Budget* (University, Ala.: Bureau of Public Administration, 1942), Chaps. 1–4; and William Vernon Holloway and Charles W. Smith, Jr., *Government and Politics in Alabama* (University, Ala.: The University Supply Store, 1941), Chap. 8.

3. *Report on a Survey of the Organization and Administration of the State and County Governments of Alabama* (Washington: The Brookings Institution, 1932), Vol. 3, Part 2, "Financial Administration of the State Government of Alabama," p. 166.

4. Ibid., p. 15.

5. *Alabama Laws,* 1932 (Extraordinary Session), No. 37.

6. *Alabama Laws,* 1976 (Regular Session), No. 257.

7. *Alabama Laws,* 1939 (Regular Session), No. 112.

8. Noted in Donald S. Vaughan, *Administrative Responsibility in Alabama* (University, Miss.: Multilith, 1967), pp. 195–96.

9. James A. Maxwell, *Financing State and Local Governments* (Washington: The Brookings Institution, 1969), pp. 216–17.

10. *Alabama Laws*, 1975 (Third Special Session), No. 108.

11. *Constitution of Alabama*, Amendment 339, approved June 10, 1975.

12. *Alabama Laws*, 1976 (Regular Session), No. 494.

Chapter Three

1. *Code of Alabama*, Title 55, Sec. 94.

2. *Constitution of Alabama*, Art. 4, Sec. 72.

3. *Opinion of Justices*, 244 Ala. 368, 13 So. (2d).

4. Coleman B. Ransone, Jr., *The Office of Governor in the South* (University, Ala.: Bureau of Public Administration, 1951), p. 85.

5. Patrick E. Nicovich, "What Happened to the Rusty Gun Behind the Door? The Non-Use of the Item Veto in Alabama" (Unpublished seminar paper, University, Alabama, Dec. 4, 1974), p. 7.

6. *Alabama Laws*, 1975 (Third Special Session), No. 108, Sec. 7.

7. *Code of Alabama*, Title 55, Sec. 102.

8. *Birmingham Post-Herald*, May 16, 1977.

9. Ibid.

10. Jerold J. Morgan, *Auditing for Alabama Governments* (University Ala.: Bureau of Public Administration, 1966), pp. 3–4. For a more detailed examination of this subject, see this work, especially Chapter 3.

11. *Constitution of Alabama*, Art. 5, Sec. 137.

12. *Code of Alabama*, Title 55, Sec. 205.

13. Ibid., Title 55, Sec. 170.

Chapter Four

1. State of Alabama, Department of Finance, *Annual Report, Fiscal Year 1975*, pp. 118–19.

2. For a more extensive discussion of state revenues, see Coleman B. Ransone, Jr., *Alabama Finances: Revenues and Expenditures, 1957–1967* (University, Ala.: Bureau of Public Administration, 1969), and Alabama Legislature, *Report of the Joint Interim Committee to Study the Tax Structure of the State of Alabama and the Distribution of Tax Revenues*, March, 1977.

3. Ira Sharkansky, *The Politics of Taxing and Spending* (Indianapolis: The Bobbs-Merrill Co., Inc., 1969), pp. 137–38.

4. For a brief description of these authorities, see Coleman B. Ransone, Jr., (ed.), *Alabama Government Manual* (University, Ala.: Bureau of Public Administration, 1977).

5. *Birmingham Post-Herald*, Sept. 27, 1975.

6. For examples of this discussion, see U.S. House of Representatives, *Message from the President of the United States Transmitting The Final Report of the Commission on Intergovernmental Relations* (The Kestnbaum Report), House Document No. 198, 84th Congress, 1st Session, 1955, pp. 129–30; and Richard E. Wagner, *The Fiscal Organization of American Federalism* (Chicago: Markham Publishing Co., 1971), Chapter 3.

Chapter Five

1. Statement of Ralph P. Eagerton, Jr., quoted in *Birmingham Post-Herald*, Feb. 5, 1976.

2. For a discussion of the pros and cons of earmarking by state governments, see James A. Maxwell, *Financing State and Local Governments* (Washington: The Brookings Institution, 1969), pp. 212–21.

3. *Constitution of Alabama*, Amendment 339, approved June 10, 1975.

4. Alabama, *Rules of the Senate of the State of Alabama*, 1975, Rule 76 (Legislative Document No. 1), p. 33.

5. *Alabama Laws*, 1976 (Regular Session), No. 763, Sections 7–14.

6. This section draws on John Ward, "The Changing Role of the State Budget Office" (Unpublished seminar paper, University, Alabama, December, 1975).

7. *Code of Alabama*, Title 55, Sec. 92.

8. Quoted in *Birmingham Post-Herald*, Aug. 27, 1975.

9. Aaron Wildavsky, *The Politics of the Budgetary Process* (Boston: Little, Brown & Company, 1974), p. 13.

10. Agencies whose budgets were selected for examination were the departments of Archives and History, Conservation and Natural Resources, Insurance, Labor, Public Safety, and Veter-ans Affairs; the State Geological Survey, State Oil and Gas Board, Bureau of Publicity and Information, and the Water Improvement Commission.

11. *Alabama Laws,* 1976 (Regular Session), No. 494.

12. Ibid., Sec. 2.

13. *Alabama Laws,* 1976 (Regular Session), No. 512.

14. Mark R. Arnold, "Sunset Budgeting," *The National Observer,* June 5, 1976, pp. 1, 19. See, also, John D. LaFaver, "Zero-Base Budgeting in New Mexico," *State Government,* Vol. 47 (Spring, 1974), 108–12.

15. The first year's experience with implementing the act was less than inspiring. During three legislative days devoted to the matter, the House considered 209 resolutions to abolish or preserve government agencies, while the Senate dealt only with 18, those agencies specifically mentioned in the law. In the end, only one agency—the Intergovernmental Cooperation Commission—was abolished. Three others recommended for termination by the review committee were preserved as a result of floor action on the resolutions.

16. Jesse Burkhead, *Government Budgeting* (New York: John Wiley and Sons, Inc., 1956), pp. 21–22.

17. Frederick C. Mosher, "Limitations and Problems of PPBS in the States," *Public Administration Review,* Vol. 29 (March/April, 1969), 165.

18. For a listing of these agencies by function, see Joseph C. Pilegge and Peter E. Jarvis, *A Program-Package Design for Alabama State Government* (Montgomery: Alabama Program Development Office, 1969) (Mimeographed).

Chapter Six

1. Allen Schick, "The Road to PPBS: The Stages of Budget Reform," *Public Administration Review,* Vol. 26 (December 1966), 243–58.

2. Paul E. Alyea, *Alabama's Balancing Budget*, (University, Ala.: Bureau of Public Administration, 1942), pp. 21, 77.

3. Jesse Burkhead, *Government Budgeting* (New York: John Wiley & Sons, Inc., 1956), p. 128.

4. Ibid., p. 130.

5. S. Kenneth Howard, *Changing State Budgeting* (Lexington, Ky.: Council of State Governments, 1973), p. 21.

6. See Allen Schick, "Control Patterns in State Budget Execution," *Public Administration Review*, Vol. 24 (June, 1964), 97–106.

7. Howard, op. cit., p. 22.

8. Allen Schick, *Budget Innovation in the States* (Washington: The Brookings Institution, 1971), Chap. 3.

9. See Jack Rabin, *Planning, Programming and Budgeting for State and Local Governments* (University, Ala.: Bureau of Public Administration, 1973); also, Robert D. Lee and Ronald W. Johnson, *Public Budgeting Systems* (Baltimore: University Park Press, 1973), Chap. 6.

10. Robert D. Calkins, "The Decision Process in Administration," *Business Horizons*, Vol. 2 (Fall, 1959), 20. See, also, Robert T. Golembiewski and Jack Rabin, *Public Budgeting and Finance* (Itasca, Ill.: F. E. Peacock Publishers, Inc., 1975) 2nd ed., Chap. 4.

11. *PPB Pilot Project Reports from the Participating 5 States, 5 Counties, and 5 Cities* (Washington: State-Local Finances Project, The George Washington University, February, 1969), p. 42.

12. Samuel M. Greenhouse, "The Planning-Programming-Budgeting System: Rationale, Language, and Idea-Relationships," *Public Administration Review*, Vol. 26 (December, 1966), 272.

13. On this point, see Allen Schick, "A Death in the Bureaucracy: The Demise of Federal PPB," *Public Administration Review*, Vol. 33 (March-April, 1973), 146–56.

14. Executive Office of the President, Office of Management and Budget, *Circular A-11*, June 21, 1971.

15. *Implementing PPB in State, City, and County* (Washington: State-Local Finances Project, The George Washington University, June, 1969), p. 11.

16. On this point, see Rabin, op. cit., pp. 28–31.

17. Schick, *Budget Innovation*, p. 104.

18. Hubert E. Pack, "Program Budgeting: Implications at the Department Level" (Address delivered at the annual Alabama State Institute on Public Administration, The University of Alabama, Mar. 23, 1976).

19. Joseph C. Pilegge and Peter E. Jarvis, *A Program-Package Design for Alabama State Government* (Montgomery: Alabama Program Development Office, 1969), (Mimeographed), p. 12.

20. Alabama Department of Finance, Division of the Budget, "What is Alabama's Program Structure?" (Montgomery: Alabama Department of Finance, 1976) (Mimeographed).

21. Pack, op. cit.

22. C. Blease Graham, "Improving State Government," *The University of South Carolina Governmental Review,* Vol. 14 (May, 1972), 3.

23. Statement of Neal E. McGowen, quoted in *Birmingham Post-Herald,* Feb. 13, 1976.

24. Associated Press dispatch, *The Tuscaloosa News,* July 29, 1976, p. 20.

25. Jere Beasley, "Accountability in State Government" (Address delivered at The University of Alabama, Oct. 28, 1976).

26. On this point, see James E. Jernberg, "Information Change and Congressional Behavior: A Caveat for PPB Reformers," *Journal of Politics,* Vol. 31 (August, 1969), 722–40.

27. See, for example, Jack Walker, "The Relation of Budgeting to Program Planning," *Public Administration Review,* Vol. 4 (Spring, 1944), 99 ff., and Frederick C. Mosher, *Program Budgeting: Theory and Practice* (Chicago: Public Administration Service, 1954), esp. pp. 47–48. For a more recent discussion, see Howard, op. cit., Chap. 7.

28. Schick, *Budget Innovation,* p. 38.

29. Ibid.

30. The Council of State Governments, *State Planning and Federal Grants* (Chicago: Public Administration Service, 1969), pp. 40–42.

31. David L. Rosebaugh, "State Planning as a Policy-Coordinative Process," *Journal of the American Institute of Planners,* Vol. 42 (January, 1976), 52–63.

32. Ernst & Ernst, *Planning-Programming-Budgeting Systems*

for State and Local Governments (Olympia, Wash.: Central Budget Agency, Planning and Community Affairs Agency, 1968), p. 22.

33. *Alabama Laws,* 1976 (Regular Session), No. 494, Sec. 2.
34. Governor's Memorandum (Accompanying budget instructions), September, 1976 (mimeographed).
35. Alabama Department of Finance, Division of the Budget, "General Instructions" (Montgomery: Alabama Department of Finance, 1976), p. 11.
36. Ibid., pp. 11–12.
37. Ibid., p. 14.
38. Robert N. Anthony, "Closing the Loop Between Planning and Performance," *Public Administration Review,* Vol. 31 (May-June, 1971), 389.
39. Alabama Department of Finance, Division of the Budget, *Chart of Expenditures, FY 1977–78* (Montgomery: Alabama Department of Finance, Sept. 1, 1976) (Mimeographed).
40. Allen Schick and Robert Keith, "Zero-Base Budgeting in the States," in U.S. Senate, Committee on Government Operations, *Compendium of Materials on Zero-Base Budgeting in the States,* 95th Congress, 1st Session, January, 1977, p. 13.

Select Bibliography

Alyea, Paul E. *Alabama's Balancing Budget.* University, Ala.:
Bureau of Public Administration, The University of Alabama,
1942.

Balutis, Alan P., and Butler, Daron K. *The Political Pursestrings:
The Role of the Legislature in the Budgetary Process.* New
York: SAGE Publications, 1975.

Buck, A. E. *The Budget in Governments of Today.* New York: The
MacMillan Co., 1934.

Budgeting by the States. Chicago: Council of State Governments,
1967.

Burkhead, Jesse. *Government Budgeting.* New York: John Wiley
& Sons, Inc., 1956.

Council of State Governments. *State Planning and Federal
Grants.* Chicago: Public Administration Service, 1969.

Golembiewski, Robert T., and Rabin, Jack. *Public Budgeting and
Finance.* 2nd ed. Itasca, Ill.: F. E. Peacock Publishers, Inc.,
1975.

Holloway, William Vernon, and Smith, Charles W. Jr. *Government and Politics in Alabama.* University, Ala.: The University
Supply Store, 1941.

Howard, S. Kenneth. *Changing State Budgeting.* Lexington, Ky.:
Council of State Governments, 1973.

Implementing PPB in State, City, and County. Washington:
State-Local Finances Project, The George Washington University, 1969.

Lee, Robert D., and Johnson, Ronald W. *Public Budgeting Systems.* Baltimore: University Park Press, 1973.

Maxwell, James A. *Financing State and Local Governments.* 2nd
ed. Washington: The Brookings Institution, 1969.

Mertins, Herman Jr., and Williams, David G. *West Virginia
Budgeting: Problems and Possibilities.* Morgantown, W. Va.:
Bureau for Government Research, West Virginia University,
1971.

Morgan, Jerold J. *Auditing for Alabama Governments.* University, Ala.: Bureau of Public Administration, The University of Alabama, 1966.

Mosher, Frederick C. *Program Budgeting: Theory and Practice.* Chicago: Public Administration Service, 1954.

PPB Pilot Project Reports from the Participating 5 States, 5 Counties, and 5 Cities. Washington: State-Local Finances Project, The George Washington University, 1969.

Rabin, Jack. *Planning, Programming and Budgeting for State and Local Governments.* University, Ala.: Bureau of Public Administration, The University of Alabama, 1973.

Ransone, Coleman B. Jr. *The Office of Governor in the South.* University, Ala.: Bureau of Public Administration, The University of Alabama, 1951.

———. *Alabama Finances: Revenues and Expenditures, 1957–1967.* University, Ala.: Bureau of Public Administration, The University of Alabama, 1969.

Schick, Allen. *Budget Innovation in the States.* Washington: The Brookings Institution, 1971.

Sharkansky, Ira. *Spending in the American States.* Chicago: Rand McNally & Company, 1968.

———. *The Politics of Taxing and Spending.* Indianapolis: The Bobbs-Merrill Co., Inc., 1969.

Thomas, James D. *Government in Alabama.* Revised ed. University, Ala.: Bureau of Public Administration, The University of Alabama, 1974.

Vaughan, Donald S. *Administrative Responsibility in Alabama.* University, Miss.: Multilith, 1967.

Wagner, Richard E. *The Fiscal Organization of American Federalism.* Chicago: Markham Publishing Co., 1971.

Wildavsky, Aaron. *The Politics of the Budgetary Process.* 2nd ed. Boston: Little, Brown & Company, 1974.

Index